GUIDELINES for

PUBLIC USE MEASUREMENT and

REPORTING at PARKS and

PROTECTED AREAS

IUCN – THE WORLD CONSERVATION UNION

Founded in 1948, The World Conservation Union brings together States, government agencies and a diverse range of non-governmental organizations in a unique world partnership: over 895 members in all, spread across some 137 countries.

As a Union, IUCN seeks to influence, encourage and assist societies throughout the world to conserve the integrity and diversity of nature and to ensure that any use of natural resources is equitable and ecologically sustainable. A central secretariat coordinates the IUCN Programme and serves the Union membership, representing their views on the world stage and providing them with the strategies, services, scientific knowledge and technical support they need to achieve their goals. Through its six Commissions, IUCN draws together over 6,000 expert volunteers in project teams and action groups, focusing in particular on species and biodiversity conservation and the management of habitats and natural resources. The Union has helped many countries to prepare National Conservation Strategies, and demonstrated the application of its knowledge through the field projects it supervises. Operations are increasingly decentralized and are carried forward by an expanding network of regional and country offices, located principally in developing countries.

The World Conservation Union builds on the strengths of its members, networks and partners to enhance their capacity and to support global alliances to safeguard naturals resources at local, regional and global levels.

WORLD COMMISSION ON PROTECTED AREAS

The World Commission on Protected Areas (WCPA), which is an integral part of IUCN – the World Conservation Union, is a world-wide network of some 1,300 protected area experts. Its members work in a volunteer capacity to raise the standard of protected areas planning and management.

The WCPA has a number of task forces, each of which tackles policy and program issues of importance to park and protected area planning and management. The objectives of the Task Force on Tourism and Protected Areas are to:

▶ Provide guidance to the WCPA, and others, on the relationships between tourism and protected areas.

▶ Identify the size and characteristics of protected area tourism.

▶ Develop case studies to investigate best practice models for tourism management.

▶ Develop guidelines for the management of tourism in protected areas.

▶ Communicate tourism management theory and practice to planners, managers and others.

▶ Provide opportunities for parks and tourism people to work together on shared issues within protected area tourism.

Pog Lake and
Campground,
Algonquin Provincial
Park, Canada

GUIDELINES for

PUBLIC USE MEASUREMENT and

REPORTING at PARKS and

PROTECTED AREAS

FIRST EDITION

AUTHORS:

KENNETH E. HORNBACK
National Park Service
United States of America

PAUL F. J. EAGLES
University of Waterloo
Canada

Safari, Ngorongoro Conservation Area, Tanzania

Keltic Lodge, Cape
Breton Highlands
National Park, Canada

WORLD
COMMISSION
ON
PROTECTED
AREAS
(WCPA)

Heron Island, Great Barrier Reef National Park, Australia

Cave and Basin Hot
Springs, Banff National
Park, Canada

Green Gables, Prince Edward Island National Park, Canada

CRC
TOURISM

Cooperative Research Centre
for Sustainable Tourism

Parcs   Parks
Canada Canada

Canadä

IUCN
The World Conservation Union

This publication has been made possible in large part by funding from Parks Canada and the Cooperative Research Centre for Sustainable Tourism of Australia.

Published by:
IUCN, Gland, Switzerland, and Cambridge, UK;
Parks Canada; Cooperative Research Centre for
Sustainable Tourism of Australia

Citation:
Hornback, Kenneth E., and Paul F.J. Eagles, 1999.
GUIDELINES FOR PUBLIC USE MEASUREMENT AND
REPORTING AT PARKS AND PROTECTED AREAS.
IUCN, Gland, Switzerland and Cambridge, UK. iv +
90 pp.

ISBN: 2-8317-0476-6

Cover photos: Paul F.J. Eagles

Designed and printed by: Graphics, University of Waterloo

Available from: IUCN Publications Services Unit
                    219c Huntingdon Road, Cambridge CB3 0DL, United Kingdom
                    Tel: ++44 1223 277894
                    Fax: ++44 1223 277175
                    E-mail: info@books.uncn.org
                    http://www.iucn.org
                    A catalogue of IUCN publications is also available

The Cooperative Research Centre for Sustainable Tourism was established as a tourism research company under the Australian Government's Cooperative Research Centre's Program, with a mission to deliver strategic knowledge to enhance the environmental, economic and social sustainability of tourism.

CRC for Sustainable Tourism
Griffith University Gold Coast
PMB 50
Gold Coast Mail Centre QLD 9726
Australia
Tel: (61-7) 5594 8172
Fax: (61-7) 5594 8171
E-mail: s.solyma@mailbox.gu.edu.au

CONTENTS

FOREWORD

The World Commission on Protected Areas (WCPA) is a Commission of the World Conservation Union (IUCN). In April 1996 the WCPA established a task force to deal with strategic objectives of tourism and protected areas. The approved objectives of the Task Force on Tourism and Protected Areas are to:

▶ Provide guidance to the WCPA, and others, on the relationships between tourism and protected areas.

▶ Identify the size and characteristics of protected area tourism.

▶ Develop case studies to investigate best practice models for tourism management.

▶ Develop guidelines for the management of tourism in protected areas.

▶ Communicate tourism management theory and practice to planners, managers and others.

▶ Provide opportunities for parks and tourism people to work together on shared issues within protected area tourism.

The absence of global data on visitor use of the world's protected area is a major policy problem. The lack of such data results in tourism being undervalued in public policy. It is difficult to understand the scale of the world's tourism use of protected areas without standard measurement units, collection procedures or integrated data management systems.

The WCPA's tourism task force moved quickly to develop procedures for the identification of the size and characteristics of tourism in the world's protected areas. This involved a three-phase project. Phase 1 was the development of definitions, approaches and standards on public use measurement and reporting for protected areas. The guidelines in this report are designed to work towards this end. Phase 2 involved the publication and distribution of the GUIDELINES to protected areas though the network of the WCPA. This alerted agency managers about the concepts and about Phase 3. Phase 3 involves the global collection of data concerning park and protected area tourism. The plan is to have the collection as part of the World Conservation Monitoring Centre's collection of data for the United Nations List of Parks and Protected Areas. The timing of the phases depends upon the funding that becomes available for the work.

You have in your hands a copy of the final version of the first edition of GUIDELINES. This version was published in English in book form and in English on the world wide web. The long-term goal is to continue to revise, refine and deepen the GUIDELINES over time. As money, time and expertise become available, the goal is to have the GUIDELINES prepared in several languages. The GUIDELINES will be published in both written and electronic format. The world wide web address that contains these GUIDELINES, and other information developed by the WCPA's tourism task force is at http://www.ahs.uwaterloo.ca/rec/taskfce.html.

ACKNOWLEDGMENTS

Thanks must go to the Australian state park agencies and the Australian Nature Conservation Agency for initiating the work on standardizing the visitor data collection procedures in that country. Their work was very useful in the preparation of these GUIDELINES. Special thanks must go the Denver Service Center of the US National Park Service. This office generously made Dr. Hornback's time available in late 1996 and early 1997 for the preparation of the first draft of this document. For some time after his retirement on March 31, 1997, the National Park Service continued to provide office space and communication facilities in the Denver office for Dr. Hornback for his work.

These GUIDELINES are the result of the contributions of many people. Jay Beaman and Dick Stanley set high standards for counting visitors in Parks Canada in recent decades. Their important fundamental contributions are acknowledged in this manual. Special thanks goes to Gene Murphy of the Federal Provincial Parks Council of Canada for circulating a draft copy of the GUIDELINES to the federal and provincial park agencies in Canada. Per Nilsen and Bill Aris of Parks Canada provided useful comments. Dr. Dan McLean of the University of Indiana circulated the Draft Guidelines to all state park agencies in the United States of America. In response, comments were received from Fran Mainella of Florida, Phillip K. McKnelly of North Carolina, Charles Van Genderen of Utah, and Jeff Erickson of Montana. Ron Seale, then working in Uganda, Norman McIntyre of Waikato University in New Zealand and Glen Hvenegaard of the Augustana University College in Alberta, Canada provided detailed comments. Robin Kruk, of the New South Wales National Parks and Wildlife Service of New South Wales, Australia, and Robin Grimwade of Centennial and Moore Park Trust, Sydney, Australia, commented on the draft GUIDELINES. Chris Haynes, Louisa Liddicoat and Wayne Schmidt, all of the Department of Conservation and Land Management of Western Australia provided a coordinated set of comments. Derek Wade, then working on visitor management in national parks in Tanzania, provided comments and case study examples from his work in Serengetti National Park. Vera Chizhova of the University of Moscow undertook the large task of translating the Draft GUIDELINES from English into Russian. She then coordinated a review by Zapovodnik managers throughout Russia. Alan Moore provided comments as well.

Kenneth J. Vrana, the Director of the Center for Maritime & Underwater Resource Management at Michigan State University in the USA prepared Chapter 7 on marine parks' tourism. Dr. Vrana encourages any questions, comments, and suggestions that may enhance future revision of information in this chapter on measurement of public use of marine protected areas. He can be contacted by e-mail at vranaken@pilot.msu.edu. In addition, Dr. Vrana acknowledges the contributions to this chapter by Dr. Daniel Stynes, Dr. Edward Mahoney, and Dr. Gail Vander Stoep of the Department of Park, Recreation and Tourism Resources at Michigan State University.

Thanks must go to the Faculty of Applied Health Sciences at the University of Waterloo, Canada. This Faculty provided the office facilities and computer resources for the preparation of the GUIDELINES and for the maintenance of the Tourism Task Force web pages. Wayne Smith and

Anne Ross, both in the Department of Recreation and Leisure Studies at the University of Waterloo, provided technical assistance for the publication.

Most photos in this publication are from the private collections of Ken Hornback and Paul Eagles. A few are from Parks Canada.

Dianne Keller and Jan Weber provided design and desktop publishing expertise to the publication.

Ken E. Hornback retired from the National Parks Service of the United States of America in 1997. For many years he was head of the social science research and visitor data collection for that agency. In that role he was responsible for the development and application of visitor data collection procedures. Ken has a PhD in Sociology from Michigan State University.

Paul F. J. Eagles is a professor in the Department of Recreation and Leisure Studies at the University of Waterloo in Ontario, Canada. He is a biologist and a planner. He has written more than 225 publications in the fields of environmental planning and park management. At the University of Waterloo he is the coordinator of the Parks Option for undergraduate students. Professor Eagles is the Co-Chair of the Task Force on Tourism and Protected Areas for the World Commission on Protected Areas. This Commission is part of the World Conservation Union, also well known by its old acronym, IUCN.

Dr. Hornback is retired from the National Park Service and is unavailable for routine comments and questions.

Please direct all comments on these GUIDELINES and suggestions for change to:

Dr. Paul F. J. Eagles
Professor
Department of Recreation and Leisure Studies
University of Waterloo
Waterloo, Ontario, Canada. N2L 3G1

Telephone 519-888-4567 extension 2716
Fax: 519-746-6776
Email: eagles@healthy.uwaterloo.ca
World Wide Web:
    http://www.ahs.uwaterloo.ca/rec/taskfce.html

Ken E. Hornback

Paul F. J. Eagles
Task Force on Tourism and Protected Areas
World Commission on Protected Areas

March 20, 1999

BACKGROUND TO PUBLIC USE REPORTING

INTRODUCTION

Park and protected area visitors are important. They have political, economic, social and ecological impacts. Much of a reserve's staff time and operational funds are dedicated to assisting, supporting and managing human use. Much of a reserve's planning and development activities are centered on human factors. The same information needed by managers is also often important to residents and business people from local communities. All of the people living on the routes traveled by park visitors will be influenced by the flow of people to and from the park.

All management is dependent upon information. The better the quality of information, the better the opportunity for good management. Information about the visitors and their activities enables managers to deal with the challenge of increasing volumes of tourism.

This manual describes terms, approaches and techniques for gathering information about public use of parks and protected areas. The goal of the manual is to supply the information necessary to meet the needs of park and protected area management in this rapidly changing field.

Parks and protected areas are unique and attract significant public interest. Public interest leads to an annual stream of visitors who invest large amounts of money, time and effort to experience these areas in person. Many factors determine the experience of visitors including; the conditions in the resource itself, the logistical support available in the park or available locally, and the attitudes

of people contacted, including the park staff and other visitors. When visitors return home, many of them become articulate and important voices favoring legislative support for existing parks and the creation of new sites. Monitoring public use is a fundamental responsibility for managers. The resulting numbers are critical indicators of the natural, social and economic functions performed by parks and their caretakers.

Sportsmen's Show, Toronto, Canada
Local tourist operators are very interested in reliable and detailed park visitation data.

The very factors that make parks and protected areas unique and exciting also make the necessary measurements of use difficult. Where great distances are involved, staff time is consumed by the logistical demands of transportation to areas where measurement takes place. Park boundaries may enclose villages and residences as well as roads and trails which necessitate the use of calculations to adjust measurements so they conform with the basic rules of reporting. The local residents near the parks and protected area may visit in high numbers but carry out activities distinctly different from foreign tourists. Such complications of the human ecology surrounding and occupying the park require careful visitor studies in addition to basic volume counts.

The GUIDELINES serve as a statistical governor which yield data to serve as reliable foundations for management and planning. As circumstances change, the GUIDELINES FOR PUBLIC USE MEASUREMENT will need modification to maintain the closest possible consistency with previous enumerations and remain comparable by adhering to standard definitions.

SOLUTIONS

The design of a public use data system at protected areas is a creative process. The designer has to balance the need for accuracy with difficult geophysical features, insufficient staff, limited funding, and competing priorities. To deal with the measurement problem most efficiently, the manager needs an inventory of options to draw from. These guidelines cover a mixture of options ranging from direct measurements with automatic counters to indirect measurements based on simple mathematical calculations. The GUIDELINES contain a kit of options which produces the most accurate and sustainable enumeration of public use of protected areas under existing circumstances.

BEST PRACTICE GUIDELINE OBJECTIVES

The objectives of the World Commission on Protected Areas' GUIDELINES FOR PUBLIC USE MEASUREMENT AND REPORTING are to:

1. Provide valid, reliable, and uniform criteria and methods for public use data collection and reporting to the independently administered parks and protected areas of member nations.

2. Identify best practices and techniques which are within the means of participating protected areas to gather regular measurements of use for local, regional, national, and international protective oversight and assistance.

3. Establish an international body of protected area use data based on consistent and comparable measurements, appropriate quality control and verification for government agencies' use in furtherance of resource and environmental protection.

Tsavo East National Park Gate, Kenya

Parks and traffic control points, such as entrance gates, have the ability to measure both the volume and length of stay of visitation.

CHAPTER 1

TERMS AND CONCEPTS

1.0 INTRODUCTION

Chapter 1 describes the basic terms and conceptual working tools for a public use information system needed by parks and protected areas. Public use information is based on statistics that comprise a limited set of data, typically actual counts, collected at regular intervals. Public use information also comes from studies consisting of sample data collected in a way that is representative of a larger population. In actual practice, public use information is based on statistics, studies, or calculations which use both statistics and study data.

1.1 DEFINITIONS OF TERMS

For the comparison of public use measurements, over time and between sites, it is necessary to adopt a standard set of definitions of the terms and concepts involved. The following definitions comprise the basic terms that describe public use of parks and protected areas. The definitions are grouped as they relate to each other, rather than in alphabetical order.

1. VISITOR: a person who visits the lands and waters of a park or protected area for purposes mandated for the area. A visitor is not paid to be in the park and does not live permanently in the park.

    Typically, the mandated purpose for the visit is outdoor recreation for natural parks and cultural appreciation for historic sites.

2. VISIT: a measurement unit involving a person going onto the lands and waters of a park or

protected area for the purposes mandated for the area.

Each visitor who enters a park for a purpose mandated for the area creates a visit statistic. Typically, the visit statistic has no length of stay data associated with it. However, the collection of additional data on the length of stay of a visit allows for the calculation of visitor hour and visitor day figures.

The purposes mandated for the area typically are recreational, educational or cultural. Non-mandated purposes could include passage through the park on the way to a site outside the park, or entrance by park maintenance vehicles. This definition of visit means that if a person leaves the park and reenters at a later time, then a second visit data unit is recorded.

3. VISITATION: the sum of visits during a period of time.

    Visitation is usually summed for use at periods, such as daily, monthly, quarterly or annually.

4. ENTRANT: a person going onto lands and waters of a park or protected area for any purpose.

    The entry figure for a park is typically larger than the visit figure. The entry figure includes data for all recreational or cultural visits as well as data for people who are in the park for activities not related to the purposes mandated for the area. For example, the entrant figure may include park visitors, plus those just driving through, local people who may pass through a corner of the park, or the daily activities of park workers. These non-visitors are usually not there for recreational or cultural purposes, but their use of park resources, such as roads, do have an impact and therefore their activities are worthy of note.

5. EXCLUSIONS: park or protected area use which is not visitation for statistical reporting purposes.

    For park management purposes, it is useful to record all entrants to the park. Later, for a variety of reasons, some types of entrants may be subtracted from, or excluded, from the figures that are reported as park use. Even though all entrants to a park have some degree of impact, there are reasons to exclude some types of use from that reported as park visits. Entries that are usually not considered park visits include traffic from commuters along major roads or railways crossing the park, traffic of attendees at non-park related activities (craft shows, races, or civil ceremonies), and traffic from residents of villages surrounded by park land. Traffic for which counts are adjusted includes traffic of individual residents, movement of park employees, volunteers working on park activities, travel of concessionaires and their employees, and the travel of trades people delivering supplies to the park. Also excluded are brief traffic across short sections of park land or waters, persons engaged in the pursuit of specific legal rights such as subsistence hunting, fishing, or native ceremonies. Sometimes law or policy dictates the type of traffic that is required to be reported, such as cruise ship passages, aircraft overflights, or commercial fishing use.

    EXAMPLES OF COMMON EXCLUSIONS INCLUDE:

    a) trips by TENANTS or RESIDENTS within park boundaries (including guests),

    b) travel by EMPLOYEES of, VOLUNTEERS at, or

    contractors to the park (including concessionaires and their employees),

    c) brief, INCIDENTAL PASSAGE into the park by pedestrian or vehicular traffic, and

    d) persons engaged in the pursuit of specific LEGAL RIGHTS OF USE (e.g., subsistence hunting and fishing, traditional ceremonies), unless there are legal or official requirements to report.

    Most excluded traffic is of a type that can be issued identification, such as with windshield stickers, to facilitate passage and to help park staff keep track of the traffic volume. It is important to keep track of the exclusions, so as to subtract this data from the total entry counts that may have been derived from manual counters such as road counters.

    For management purposes, data on the exclusions can be useful in its own right. For example, tenants at private cottages in the park may use the roads. Knowledge of this use is important for maintenance purposes. Similarly, data of the levels of subsistence fishing in the waters of the park is needed for fisheries management purposes. Therefore, it is important that all data on all use be documented.

    In high use areas it may be difficult to detect recreational use from activities normally excluded. Visitor studies of a sample of the park users may be necessary to ascertain the reasons for use.

6. CALCULATIONS: determining or refining visitation by mathematical conversion of counts, partial counts, study data, recorded observations or judgement. Common types of calculations are given below.

    a) ADJUSTMENT, meaning a change of a visitation or entries count to remove exclusions, e.g., a traffic count might be reduced by 25% to adjust for local traffic that is just passing through.

b) CORRECTION, meaning a change of an instrument reading to reflect error that has been determined by independent calibration (by visual, multiple instrument counting, etc.).

c) CONSTANT, meaning a fixed number for minor volumes of activity determined by a one-time measurement, a special study, or the judgement by staff.

d) APPROXIMATION, meaning a number assigned to an uncounted area based on measurements at nearby or comparable areas, where studies have determined the relationship between the two sites.

e) ESTIMATE, meaning a number derived from a methodical computation based on regular, but partial, counts. An example is a figure of 2.3 persons per car, an estimate based on a 1 week sample gate count collected at the beginning of the peak season.

f) SUBSTITUTION, meaning the use of a previously recorded number for an area when current data are temporarily unavailable, for example when the traffic counter is temporarily broken. An example might be the use of the number from the same month the previous year.

g) CONVERSION, meaning the change of a number from one indicator to another. Several conversions are typically made. It is common to convert from visitor hours to visitor days, for example one person may stay for 4 hours, which converts to .33 visitor days when one is using a definition of 12 hours for a visitor day. Another conversion is from visitor nights to visit days. Since many campers or lodge users stay for an entire 24 hour period, it is common to equate one visitor night, of 24 hours, as being equal to one visitor day of 12 hours. Many agencies simply count the number of entrants to a park, without recording the length of stay for each entrant and without checking to see if the entrant is really a visitor. To convert entrants to visits, it is necessary to find the number of entrances that are not related to the park. This can be done by sampling the stream of traffic entering the park and asking the people the reasons for their entry. Once the sample data is obtained, the percentage of entrances that are really visits can be calculated, then multiplied by the entire entrance data set to get the actual visitor numbers. Similar logic can be applied to finding visitor hours. Sample surveys of visitors can be done to find the average length of stay. This average length of stay can then be multiplied by the total visit figure to get visitor hours.

7. COUNT: the direct observation and immediate recording, measurement by instrument, or recording by registration form (such as fee collections) of park or protected area use.

8. VISITOR NIGHTS: the count of persons staying overnight in a park or protected area for a purpose mandated for the area.

Typically people stay in the park either in a lodge or in a camping area. Many parks record data on such use as bed nights or camper nights, figures comparable to visitor nights.

9. ENTRY NIGHTS: the count of persons staying overnight in a park or protected area for any purpose.

Entry nights data are larger than visitor nights data. Entry nights include all visitor nights, plus the nights of people who are not visitors. For example, entry nights might include the data of overnight stays of park staff or concessionaire employees.

10. VISITOR HOURS: the total length of time, in hours, (both continuous and intervals) that visitors stay in the park while visiting for a purpose mandated for the area.

11. ENTRY HOURS: the total length of time, in hours, (both continuous and intervals) that visitors and entrants stay in the park for any purpose.

12. VISITOR DAY: the total number of days that visitors stay in the park.

The visitor day figure illustrates levels of park use. It is calculated for comparative purposes between sites and between time periods. Visitor day data can be recorded directly from the visitors. For example, in some parks all visitors sign in and sign out of the park, thereby providing very accurate records on length of stay. However, such precise data is rare. Therefore, the visitor day figure is usually calculated from visit figures multiplied by the length of park stay. The length of stay is often an average figure derived from visitor surveys of a sample of visitors. A "visitor day" is often defined as 12 "visitor hours" of park use, however this varies amongst agencies. The total visitor day data is generated by the addition of various lengths of stay. Small parks and historic parks may have short average lengths of stay, say 3 hours, which means that it will take several visits to add up to one "visitor day." Large national parks often have long periods of stay, say 3 days, which means that a single visit constitutes more than one "visitor day." The visitor day indicator makes a comparison possible between historical and natural sites, between different park systems and between different countries.

13. TOURIST: a person travelling to and staying in a place outside their usual environment for not more than one consecutive year for leisure, business and other purposes.

The definition of a tourist involves two elements, travel of a certain distance from home and a length of stay. For most parks a portion of the visitors will be tourists, the rest being considered local residents. It is often useful for the park's visitor management personnel to report on the percentage of park visitors that are tourists.

The definition of tourist varies amongst countries. Consultation with the national tourism body is necessary to ensure that the collection of visitor data from a park can be done in a way that is consistent with the collection of tourism data for the country.

1.2 CONSISTENCY WITH NATIONAL TOURISM STATISTICS

It is important that data on park visitors be defined and collected in such a way that it is consistent with the broader tourism data collected for the country. For example, one key aspect of the definition of a tourist, is the length of travel from home to the visitation site. However, this varies. Canada typically uses an 80-km distance (50 miles), but the USA typically uses 160 km (100 miles). Therefore, the designers of data collection effort in a park system need to be aware of both the national and the international approaches. The World Tourism Organization developed guidelines on international tourism. These guidelines were subsequently adopted by the United Nations Statistical Committee and published in report format. Appendix 1, at the back of this report, contains a more complete set of tourism definitions.

1.3 USES OF PUBLIC USE DATA BY MANAGERS

The scope and level of effort put into the public use measurement program should be in proportion to the requirement of park managers to provide for general management, natural resource protection, maintenance operations and visitor services and protection. Examples of the role of visitation data in these categories are explained below.

GENERAL MANAGEMENT

All managers need quantitative data on how visitation impacts the park or protected area and qualitative data on how the park or protected area impacts the visitor. Moreover, managers need to know these conditions internally as well as immediately outside the park or protected area.

Visitation data are needed to compute statistical reports (rate per thousand) on sanitation, public health, accident, fire suppression, criminal acts, search and rescue missions, etc. These data have expensive consequences and are especially important during the government budgetary process.

Current volume gives an idea of the popularity of various activities and services monitored at the point of delivery from roadside display utilization to interpretive programs attendance, concessionaire provided guide, boat or livery service demand, and other similar activities.

Measurements from zones of use and avenues of access indicate optimal fee collection locations as well as allocation of staff resources and possible staging of facilities and services.

Current public use volumes, overnight stays by type, rate of change, comparisons to other local areas, and related data are of value to local residents, officials, businesses, as well as to other agencies and to general government functions. All people who must plan for the park visitation must have good data.

Visitation data are convertible into economic consequences (tourism sales, jobs, taxes) and help evaluate the value of the park and park resources in common terms with other activities (agricultural, mining, etc.). Visitation data provide useful insight for people who might otherwise not care or understand the influence of the park to them and their economic life.

When unusual events occur and an idea of impacts on visitation is needed to deal with unexpected consequences or emergencies, accurate and comparable historical data is suddenly crucial. In other words, current visitation data may become critical important at some later point in time.

NATURAL RESOURCE PROTECTION

The protection and management of natural resources is an important activity. Visitor use has a direct and immediate impact on a park or protected area's natural environment. Of special interest is any subsistence-based resource use, such as may occur by local residents.

Knowledge of public use activity, location and volume is needed to evaluate and preserve viable natural ecosystems, including endangered and threatened plant and animal species. It is very important to help manage wildlife habitats, prevent human-wildlife interaction problems, protect range, migration patterns, resting and nesting sites, and maintain vegetative cover, soil surfaces, and water quality within desirable limits.

Knowledge of planned public use activity, location and volume is necessary to evaluate, protect, preserve and maintain cultural sanctuaries (spiritual grounds), archaeological ruins and historical structures.

Attention paid to visitor volume leads to better awareness of general visitor behavior, from cutting firewood to unsanitary personal hygiene, which creates a hazard for the resource as well as other visitors. As a result, preventive measures ranging from signs to facility construction can be taken.

Some visitors will go exploring off park roads and trails. As they leave traces for others to notice, new trails emerge. Resource managers must know total use, use at planned sites and unplanned visitation around critical sites. They must watch for, detect, and deal with drifting internal use patterns. Fractional changes can lead to rapid impacts on fragile resources, sensitive wildlife, migratory zones or delicate habitats and require immediate deterrent measures. Visitation rates, rates at sensitive areas, known peak loads at nearby areas, and records of resource wear at certain volumes must be regularly analyzed to protect and maintain the natural resources within the limits of acceptable change, i.e., in a manner that ensures the damage is minimal and repairable.

MAINTENANCE OPERATIONS

While maintenance operations can be performed after damage is evident, preventive maintenance operations require a knowledge of visitor use levels. This section describes some of these operations.

Public use volume and short-term forecasts of use are needed to order supplies and maintain minimal inventory of consumables (soap, toilet paper, paint, gasoline, etc.).

Public use volume at specific service areas (campground landscape, firepits, benches, tables, roads and trails, parking and staging areas, etc.) is needed for daily repair, maintenance and replacement budgeting and scheduling.

Current, peak and seasonal volume at each major development (hardened resources, facilities and functional areas, e.g., parking, staging, road, trail, etc.) is examined for changes in utilization rates relative to capacity, age and useful facility life cycle, changing rates of routine maintenance and replacement cost programming or associated consequences of prolonged use.

Records of public use volume, visual evidence of excessive wear and associated costs are evaluated to determine when the continuous cost of labor for preventive maintenance (caused by poor design, materials and construction) exceeds the capital costs of redesign and reconstruction or the costs of redeployment of visitation through general park use planning.

Park staff need to be assigned on the basis of internal concentrations of visitor activity for cleanup and hasty repair. Assignments need to be made in sufficient strength, with the right equipment, at the right time to limit public complaints.

Visitor use data are used for road capacity planning and design. Of special interest are data associated with locally originating traffic which might only use certain sections of longer passageways.

VISITOR SERVICES AND PROTECTION

The provision of visitor services is dependent on the needs and numbers of visitors, availability of funds, and resource protection concerns, e.g., site hardening, pollution abatement, etc.

Establishing and maintaining public use safety and sanitation standards must be conducted in ratio to actual volume (water quality sampling and treatment, waste removal, etc.).

Daily operational service level standards (especially instructional directives to visitors and changes in monitoring and patrol functions) need to be made according to use volume as it relates to season, current temperature conditions (extreme heat, cold, weather turnabouts), resource conditions (fire hazard warning and restrictions) and wildlife control activities (preventive measures associated with unusual disease threats).

Public use monitoring activities put park staff in a position to detect, control and correct restricted or illegal activities (poaching, removal of artifacts, destruction of plant materials, etc.).

The park may have legal liability exposure during certain times of use, such as periods of very high use or times of participation in dangerous activities. The volume and timing of such activities needs to be known, communicated to appropriate people and contingency plans made.

Visibility of park staff during various public use monitoring activities has a secondary benefit of deterring vandalism.

Public use monitoring activities make staff accessible to the public to address needs or provide impromptu environmental education.

Public use monitoring activities help to ensure that adequate volumes of materials required for public distribution can be ordered and sufficient inventory maintained.

The provision of interpretive programs and information services is frequently tied to anticipated visitor numbers based on records of previous volumes measured.

All these basic areas of work are subject to the availability of resources! If resources for measuring and monitoring public use are insufficient, it is the responsibility of the area manager to identify how this management function (and other resource protection functions) cannot be performed and inform the supporting agencies and officials.

1.4 THE PROBLEM OF UNDER-REPORTING

Many parks do not count visitation effectively. This may be due to low levels of staffing, too many entrances for proper coverage, or other priorities of management. Some park systems only count visitation at those parks with the highest levels of use. Many systems report zero levels of use from some periods and some parks. All of this results in under reporting of visitation. Under-reporting gives a misleading impression in government, in the public and in business about the level of use of a park and of a parks' system. This in turn can lead to lower levels of policy emphasis in government and to depressed budget levels. It is much better to develop a simple, but reasonably accurate, public use measurement system that provides an estimate or count of visitation, than to make the mistake of not counting at all.

Great Smoky Mountains National Park, USA

Great Smoky Mountains National Park has one of the highest visitation figures for national parks in the world. This important fact is known because of a sophisticated public use measurement and reporting system.

CHAPTER 2

PROGRAM DEVELOPMENT: FROM INITIAL TO ADVANCED

2.0 PROGRAM DEVELOPMENT

The discussion of program development in Chapter 2 is intended to show how public use can be monitored and useful data be collected at a variety of progressive levels, going from a simple situation to a complex park with specialized visitor management programs. Any park or protected area can start to monitor public use at a reasonable level of accuracy and reliability regardless of staff or funding support. The overview in Chapter 2 makes use of techniques and methods that are discussed in detail by later chapters of these GUIDELINES. Area managers are encouraged to take one step at a time, starting with an initial level program and improving it as needs dictate.

Even the most elementary level of public use reporting represents some investment of park staff effort for: (1) collecting data, (2) summarization of data, (3) analysis of data, and (4) interpretation of data for management action. The exact size of the investment made by the park or protected area in monitoring public use depends on the needs of management and the number of functions there are to be served.

There are five progressive levels of public use program advancement described in this report starting with an INITIAL LEVEL (I) of public use reporting program and moving on to BASIC (II), INTERMEDIATE (III), DEVELOPED (IV) and ADVANCED (V) levels. Each higher level results in greater accuracy and detail of public use data and a corresponding increase in required staff time, hardware and funding.

The development of a program for public use reporting involves a progression through the levels for three reasons. First, parks vary in complexity of boundaries, access points, composition of natural and human ecology, development of facilities, and the extent of use and degrees of impact. The public use reporting program varies correspondingly. Some parks will be well served by lower level programs than others for the present. Times change and so must reporting programs. Second, to the extent that a program grows along with the needs of the park staff for management data, the program will tend to be carefully administrated and developed to higher levels of accuracy. If staff do not trust or understand the data, they will never use or learn to use it. As this learning occurs, more and better data will be demanded and the program will be changed to meet the increased demand. Third, it is, unfortunately, too easy to create a program of reporting which is unnecessarily complicated, especially if the data collectors are not the main data users. Central office personnel are often asked by parks to simplify counting programs that have been created by the parks themselves . . . usually by previous employees. Even parks that are already counting public use are encouraged to review their efforts and redevelop their efforts with careful attention to the balance of effort and the applicability of data to park management.

Long-term accuracy is a balance of precision and practicality. If a program is too complicated to be practically applied in the park, it cannot be sustained. An overly complicated program will ultimately become problematic.

Park entrance at Banff National Park, Canada

Controlled entrance procedures can be used for the collection of significant amounts of data on park entrants and visitors.

Parks that collect fees for all visits have the opportunity to collect substantial amounts of visitor data, easily and simply. Such parks often have point of sale (P.O.S.) computer terminals. These terminals automatically collect the time of the visit, the day and the type of entry (adult, family, school, child, senior, etc.) of each sale. The system is very precise and allows for almost immediate data on the level of visitation and some of the characteristics of this visitation. The point of sale data collection works best with single or only a few points of entry. The data from such procedures allow managers to analyze their data in many ways that were not possible in the past. These procedures have often eliminated previous methodologies such as hand counts, registration books, visual counts and optical sensors at some locations. The results are highly accurate, yet require minimal additional staff time because gate staff are already collecting entry fees. Parks at the advanced levels sometimes ask visitors for their postal codes, enabling geographical analysis of visitation and cross-tabulation with many existing market surveys.

2.1 THE SETTING

To develop the background to a public use measurement program, a hypothetical example is presented. The imaginary Mangrove Protected Area (Figure 1) has two areas where staff contact visitors, a small contact station (visitor center and headquarters) and a campground. Camping fees are collected. There is only one staff person. The staff is assigned to the visitor center most of the day, but makes a tour of the campground during the last hour of the work day. Campers pay their fee and register at either the visitor center or campground. Campers must fill out a registration form and receive a receipt for display at the campsite. A road runs through the park. Entrances are not monitored. There is roadside parking for a trail head and an overlook.

Six kinds of use occur. People can go to the visitor center but not to the campground. They can go to the campground and skip the visitor center. They can visit the park and skip both the visitor center and campground. They can visit the visitor center, campground, and park. They can also drive through the park without stopping. Finally, the park is visited by a number of government employees who are excluded from counts for statistical purposes.

FIGURE 1: MANGROVE PROTECTED AREA

2.2 LEVEL I: THE INITIAL PUBLIC USE REPORTING PROGRAM

Any park can count visitation, even if it is on a partial or limited basis. In fact, a good way to build a program is by observing and learning about how a park works on the basis of actual use.

2.2.1 WHAT IS REPORTED AT LEVEL I

The INITIAL counting program at Mangrove Protected Area consists of a staff person with a hand counter keeping track of people who enter the visitor center during the day. While in the visitor center, visitors can register to stay in the campground. Registered campers are issued a display tag as a receipt from a registration form that is kept on file. During the evening campground check, the staff person makes a tour of the campground to check the display tags of registered campers. People who show up in the campground without registration are registered at that time.

The registration forms from additional campers are collected in the evenings and entered into the visitor center log the next morning as additional overnight stays. A separate count is recorded for day visitors and the number of visitors registered to stay overnight (Table 1).

The counts of visits (day use and overnight) are multiplied by the constants in use for length of stay to convert them to visitor hours. In this case those constants are based on staff judgement that day users spend 8 hours in the park and that overnight users spend 24 hours in the park. Statistics are compiled monthly and a historical record of seasonal variations is started.

2.2.2 SHORTCOMINGS OF LEVEL I

With a Level I system, generally the staff person is aware of only a small amount of park use and has no idea of patterns (day use, overnight stays, excluded traffic, traffic in either direction or pass through or turnabouts). After a few weeks of doing counts this way the problems become apparent:

▶ People who show up at the campground may or may not have been in the visitor center. Some of these "new" registrants, however, seem to be recognized as visitor center visitors from earlier in the day (indicating a double count if one knew for sure).

▶ Traffic is seen passing by the front of the visitor center which doesn't stop and isn't counted.

▶ There is no way to tell the difference between visits, entries and other traffic (i.e., potentially excluded use).

TABLE 1: WHAT IS REPORTED IN A LEVEL I (INITIAL PUBLIC USE REPORTING PROGRAM)

	REPORTED	METHOD
Visits	YES	MC
Corrected for Counter Error?	Not applicable	
Adjusted for Excluded Use?	NO	
Adjusted for Entries?	NO	
Visitor Hours	YES	CS
Entries	NO	
Visitor Nights	YES	MC
Visitor Night Hours	YES	CC-Reg. Forms
Entry Night Hours	NO	

MC = Manual Count	AC = Automated Count	ES = Estimate (partial count)	AD = Adjustment
CS = Constant	CV = Conversion	CC = Calculation	AP = Approximation

▶ Traffic entering the park from the south entrance are not counted.

▶ Traffic entering before or after the staff tour of duty is unknown.

▶ The accuracy, volume and duration of stay of day use is unknown.

▶ An entire group of visitors may not enter the visitor center and may not be counted.

▶ Records that are kept on a daily basis and compiled monthly are prone to clerical errors. This is especially true when calculations are involved. Unless there is some independent and reliable checking of calculations, errors are likely to accumulate and compound in later reports. If reporting errors are not corrected immediately there are seldom enough records or recollection to correct them later.

▶ Counting of registration forms and calculation of items from separate records (visitor center log is updated from the registration forms collected) is error-prone.

▶ The staff person in the visitor center can keep track of public use for only short periods between interruptions to answer questions and register people for camping.

▶ The use of hand counters is error prone.

2.2.3 BENEFITS OF LEVEL I

The Level I program is low in cost and is administered as time permits. While there are few management benefits from such a partial counting program, it is a start. Even this initial program will help staff become familiar with record keeping and the need for attention to detail. This initial counting experience will lead to ideas about program improvements. It is easy to see in this example how an apparently simple arrangement can get complicated. It is better for a park to establish a reporting program with such initial simplicity than to design a more comprehensive program and then learn how difficult it can be to administer.

2.3 LEVEL II: THE BASIC PUBLIC USE REPORTING PROGRAM

The difference between the INITIAL and BASIC program is experience and ingenuity. Initially, the park layout and staff assignments will dictate a program that is feasible under the circumstances. The INITIAL program is driven by what can be done as opposed to any notion of what should be done. As staff gain experience with such initial practices, they will develop an awareness of the limitations of such a system and the errors that can be made. Those involved will observe and form impressions or speculations about actual park use that suggest changes from the initial plan for reporting. While additional resources may not yet be available to the park, there are always steps to improve the INITIAL program. What is surprising is that often those steps are not taken.

Bruce Peninsula National Park/
Fathom Five National Marine Park
Visitor Centre, Canada

Visitor Centres are often used as contact points for special visitor surveys.

Experience with the INITIAL program at Mangrove Protected Area leads the staff to some ideas about what to change. Here are the changes made to improve the initial program and bring it up to the BASIC or Level II program.

▶ People who show up at the campground without registration may or may not have been in the visitor center where their presence would be counted as a visit. The confusion about going to the visitor center and registering for overnight use can be resolved by altering the campground registration form to include use of the visitor center (yes or no). This will eliminate under-counts. Campground users who answer no (they did not use the visitor center) are added to the visitor center count of overnight visits and to visits. Over-counts will also be eliminated. Campground users who answer yes (they did use the visitor center) will be added to the visitor center overnight count but not to visits.

▶ Traffic can be seen passing by the front of the visitor center which doesn't stop and isn't counted. Some of this traffic may be through traffic (which does not stop in the park) or visitors who are not interested in going to the visitor center. To deal with the volume of pass-by traffic some informal observations could

be made for the first 5 minutes of each hour from the visitor center window. Careful records (informal does not mean haphazard) from these observations will give an evenly distributed, daily sample of 40 minutes (5 minutes times an 8-hour shift) before leaving to patrol the campground. By multiplying the observed pass-by traffic times 12 (480 minutes in an 8-hour shift divided by 40 minutes of observation), an approximation can be made of the park activity which is not recorded in the visitor center. A methodical computation (estimate) is better than a guess or omission.

2.3.1 WHAT IS REPORTED AT LEVEL II

Although there is no change at the BASIC level program in what is reported, significant improvements have been made in how data are collected. The over- and under-reporting that was part of the INITIAL program has been reduced (Table 2).

Pass-by traffic remains a problem, although there is now an estimate of the volume. It is still unclear how much of this traffic is visitation, excluded use, or pass-through traffic. However, if the volume is large or if there are other indicators of resource problems, this deficiency of management information will have to be resolved by making further improvements in public use reporting.

TABLE 2: WHAT IS REPORTED AT LEVEL II (BASIC PUBLIC USE REPORTING PROGRAM)

		REPORTED	METHOD
Visits		YES	MC
	Corrected for Counter Error?	Not applicable	
	Adjusted for Excluded Use?	NO	
	Adjusted for Entries?	NO	
Visitor Hours		YES	CS
Entries		NO	
Visitor Nights		YES	MC
Visitor Night Hours		YES	CC-Reg. Forms
Entry Night Hours		NO	

MC = Manual Count   AC = Automated Count   ES = Estimate (partial count)   AD = Adjustment
CS = Constant   CV = Conversion   CC = Calculation   AP = Approximation

2.3.2 SHORTCOMINGS OF LEVEL II

▶ There is no way to tell the difference between visits, entries and other traffic (i.e., excluded).

▶ Traffic entering the park from the south entrance are not counted.

▶ Traffic entering before or after the staff tour of duty is unknown.

▶ The accuracy, volume and duration of stay of day-use is unknown.

▶ An entire group of visitors may not enter the visitor center and may not be counted.

▶ Records that are kept on a daily basis and compiled monthly are prone to clerical errors. This is especially true when calculations are involved. Unless there is some independent and reliable checking of calculations, errors are likely to accumulate and compound in later reports. If reporting errors are not corrected immediately, there are seldom enough records or recollection to correct them later.

▶ Counting of registration forms and calculation of items from separate records (visitor center log is updated from the registration forms collected) is error-prone.

▶ The staff person in the visitor center can keep track of public use for only short periods between interruptions to answer questions and register people for camping.

▶ The use of hand counters is error-prone.

2.3.3 BENEFITS OF LEVEL II

Two shortcomings of the INITIAL program have been improved at the BASIC level through the ingenuity and efforts of park staff. More has been learned about additional sources of reporting error and the need for more complete data for future resource management and park operations decisions. By progressing to the BASIC Level II program, the park is in a better position to demonstrate why it needs additional support to improve the public use reporting program.

2.4 LEVEL III: INTERMEDIATE PUBLIC USE REPORTING PROGRAM

As a result of Level II efforts, some resources in the form of funding become available to the park. There are many ways to improve the Mangrove Protected Area program. This improvement can lead to a Level III, or INTERMEDIATE program.

Each staff person will have suggestions about improvements based on their individual experience and point of view. A common improvement that first comes to mind is to buy traffic counters to place on the roads around the park. Road counters would certainly relieve the staff of some of the counting and record keeping. The problem with this solution is that visitors may not be doing what the park staff believe they are doing. In addition, there may be ways of making estimates of use for certain areas without counters. In any case, the funding may not be enough to put counters (or read and maintain counters) in all the places staff think they should go. Purchasing and installing counting instruments may be the first idea that comes to mind but it is not always the best, next step in improving a public use reporting program. For example, a common problem is that once road counters are installed, they will probably stay where they have been put! If the counters are in a poor locale, they may be recording inappropriate or misleading data.

To develop a program to the INTERMEDIATE program, Level III, more basic descriptive information about visitors is needed. Such information often comes from a visitor survey. Surveys are studies designed to represent all visitors within a certain time period. Surveys use questionnaires to produce sets of data that accurately describe the visitors, their visits, and their travel to the park. Detailed and accurate data about visitor use will help determine the most cost-effective locations where counting instruments should be placed as well as measure factors needed to apply instrument counts to reportable park use. The survey will measure the patterns of use (from point of entry to exit), identify the statistical relationships between the basic areas of use (visitor center, campground, overlook, trail head, and entrances), and produce factors needed for reporting (identification of the amount of excluded use as well as measure entries). The survey will also indicate areas and patterns of use that have important similarities or differences, e.g., day users and overnighters, local visitors or non-local visitors, large versus small groups.

A visitor survey is designed to gather data during short exit interviews conducted for one hour samples at different time periods on randomly chosen days of the study month (survey methods are further described in Chapter 4). A count of passing vehicular traffic is kept so the sample can be expanded to indicate the entire park use for that month (Table 3). These data must be collected from a random sample of visitors. If these data come from a random sample, they are representative of all visitors for the period under investigation.

The design and administration of a visitor survey will enable several shortcomings of the Level II program to be resolved:

▶ What is the exact volume of basic categories of visitors: visitors, entries, and excluded traffic? A question about the purpose of the trip through the park should clearly establish the difference between visit, entry, and any activity which is excluded from statistical reporting.

▶ What is the relative volume of traffic past the two entrances? This can be resolved in a number of ways. The locations where visitors are contacted can be alternated between the two entrances. If the staff numbers permit, a concurrent study at each location could be conducted. Separate pretests of the questions to be asked on the survey could be conducted and estimates of the relative use based entirely on the pretest.

▶ What is the volume of traffic entering before or after the staff tour of duty? It is seldom practical to answer this question for 24 hours of the day. However, survey hours can be staggered to cover several hours before and after normal tours of duty to estimate the volume of off-hour traffic.

▶ What is the exact length of stay in the park of visitors? A question addressing date and time of entrance and exit establishes length of stay. In cases where there may be some doubt about exits and re-entries, the question about exit may be phrased "are you leaving the park for the last time this trip?"

▶ The visitor survey includes a question about going to the visitor center. Answers to this question can be used to determine a percentage by which visitor center counts are increased to reflect the number of people who don't go inside.

During the design of the survey, some thought needs to be given to future data needs. In the next level of program development it is possible that automatic counting instruments will be needed.

TABLE 3: CALCULATING TOTAL VISITATION BASED ON SURVEY DATA

Assume a 30-day month of 12 hour, dawn-to-dusk days or 360 possible hours of sampling.	The 21 hours of sampling are 5.8% of the monthly total (21/360) so the pass-by traffic at the sampling site are 5.8% of the total traffic count assuming negligible traffic at night.	In Stage I the percentage of the monthly visitor center count gives a rough estimate of the year. If the peak month estimate is known, the remainder of the year can be calculated.

With that possibility in mind, the survey needs to be broad enough in scope and design to uncover in detail how people use the park and where they go. It is important to remember that a part of the joy of park visitation is exploration and to that extent the survey must be open to new information people have to give about their explorations.

2.4.1 WHAT IS REPORTED AT LEVEL III

At Level III the park has a comprehensive estimate of public use of the entire park, at least for one period of time. The complexities of park uses are now known including local day visits, non-local visits, visitation and total entries, overnights, and visitor hours. Most importantly, the full volume of park use can be estimated because the number who slip past the counters at the visitor center or campground can be estimated from survey data. At this point the park can use the survey results to create an estimate of park use for any management application during the sample period. The Level III program produces visitor use data that is reliable enough to be useful in many aspects of park management.

The task of manual computation of overnight stay hours from registration forms is replaced by an average length of stay based on the survey. The estimated day-use hours are also based on the survey.

The peak month sample can be expanded to an estimate of the entire month. With a much higher risk of error, the month can be expanded to represent the periods immediately before and after the data collection, but probably not the entire season (depending on what that is). Unfortunately, the relationships indicated from the survey data can probably not be counted on to persist throughout the year. The only way to know that is to conduct regular surveys, such as bimonthly or seasonally. Quarterly surveys are recommended as a minimum until enough survey data are available to indicate otherwise.

While the survey is the main distinction of an INTERMEDIATE Level III program, it is also the basis for making the transition to a DEVELOPED, Level IV, program to be discussed later.

2.4.2 SHORTCOMINGS OF LEVEL III

In a Level III program several of the original shortcomings have been corrected. The park is now able to operate on the basis of a broad knowledge of the volume of use that must be supported. Unfortunately, improved as they may be, refinements of the data are based on extrapolations, estimates, and proportions from a survey at only one point in time.

TABLE 4: WHAT IS REPORTED AT LEVEL III (INTERMEDIATE PUBLIC USE REPORTING PROGRAM)

		REPORTED	METHOD
Visits		YES	MC
	Corrected for Counter Error?	Not applicable	
	Adjusted for Excluded Use?	YES	Survey
	Adjusted for Entries?	YES	Survey
Visitor Hours		YES	Survey
Entries		YES	Survey
Visitor Nights		YES	MC & Survey
Visitor Night Hours		YES	Survey Avg.
Entry Night Hours		YES	Survey

MC = Manual Count   AC = Automated Count   ES = Estimate (partial count)   AD = Adjustment
CS = Constant   CV = Conversion   CC = Calculation   AP = Approximation

Most parks will need more than a single visitor survey to represent the full range of visitor use over the cycle of a year as seasons and activities change. The data indicated from a visitor survey may only be good for the particular portion of the year in which the survey was conducted. It is highly risky to base general management decisions (resource, maintenance or any other kind) on a single study or month of data.

▶ The corrections that have been made are based on a single survey whose data are representative of that month only.

A respectable level of administrative skill is needed to summarize and use survey data in conjunction with periodical public use reporting. At this level, the work is spread out to individuals with time available. The nature of this work has grown to a level of complexity that does not lend itself to informal assignments as time permits. While the overall scope of public use reporting has improved, the risk of error in preparing data has increased.

▶ The system in use has become complicated and requires attention to detail, prior experience, administrative skills and a block of uninterrupted time for verification of calculations.

Several previous shortcomings remain:

▶ Records that are kept on a daily basis and compiled monthly are prone to clerical errors. This is especially true when calculations are involved. Unless there is some independent and reliable checking of calculations, errors are likely to accumulate and compound in later reports. If reporting errors are not corrected immediately, there are seldom enough records or recollection to correct them later.

▶ Counting of campground registration forms and calculation of items from separate records is error-prone.

▶ The staff person in the visitor center can keep track of public use for only short periods between interruptions to answer questions and register people for camping.

▶ The use of hand counters is error prone.

▶ It is possible that the visitor surveys did not collect a random sample of park visitors, thereby causing a sampling error and leading to erroneous conclusions.

2.4.3 BENEFITS OF LEVEL III
At the INTERMEDIATE level of public use reporting the needs of park operation, resource protection and visitor services functions can be served accurately for the sampled period and at a gross level for the rest of the year. As respect and the need for reliable data grow, so will the understanding that the standards for careful work apply to all areas of park work: maintenance records, resource management records, as well as public use records. To the extent that the general

Valley of the Giants Tree Top Walk at Valley of the Giants, Walpole-Nornalup National Park, Western Australia

Special visitor facilities, such as elevated walkways, attract high levels of use. Such facilities are excellent sites for point of sale data collection.

importance of monitoring the park grows, the interest in moving to a Level IV program will spread throughout the staff. Needless to say, changing conditions, especially public use, will drive general staff interest in resource monitoring to the point of anxiety. The faster park use is changing, the sooner a single visitor survey becomes outdated.

At Level III a visitor survey is conducted rather than installation of new counters. Data from counters has its limitations that should be recognized. However, the use data from one or more counters as well as data from the visitor survey will give a much improved picture of reality.

2.5 LEVEL IV: DEVELOPED PUBLIC USE REPORTING PROGRAM

With a DEVELOPED program the park will have sufficient resources and staff to administrate and support a public use reporting program at a level of accuracy that will serve the needs of all operational departments including planning and budget.

At the DEVELOPED level program three major actions are taken to raise the park or protected area from the INTERMEDIATE level:

▶ The visitor survey is replicated for as many seasons as management determines is appropriate or until no significant variation in data between seasons remain. Seasonal adjustments can be made to the automated instrument system to generate public use data and estimates for all areas of park use including entries and exclusions.

▶ The administration of the overall system has passed from a few personnel performing other duties as assigned to a staff person with specialized skills who controls all aspects of the program (instrumentation, operation, compilation and reporting) including consultancy to other operational departments

for their public use and visitor data needs. Any errors are the responsibility of a specific person.

▶ Instrumentation is installed where appropriate and cost effective based on an analysis of visitors and their traffic through the park. At a minimum, this means an optical sensor to count visitor center traffic and entrance station traffic counters. Errors from hand counters and staff trying to do two jobs at one time are eliminated.

There are, however, two remaining concerns at the DEVELOPED level: improving the accuracy of public use data and reducing the labor intensive work of collecting and processing reports on the data.

If funding is limited, traffic counter sensors can be placed where needed. One traffic counter can serve more than one sensor by being rotated from location to location. The data reported become estimates based on partial counts. In the case of Mangrove Protected Area, the availability of at least one traffic counter will add a partial count for the north entrance and south entrance (Figure 2).

A DEVELOPED, or Level IV, program has at least one staff dedicated to the task, rather than depending on the services of momentarily unassigned individuals. This person has public use measurement as a primary part of their job assignment. They should have specialized training in survey design, data collection, data management, statistics and report writing. The assignment of staff to the public use reporting function is warranted by growing demands for accurate data by other operating divisions of the park management (resource protection, visitor health and safety, maintenance). Those other users of visitor data may also have additional needs for data requiring further development of the program. The campground staff, for example, may want to know the exact volume of traffic that is turning off the main road into their site. The general park program does not require that kind of detail, but if it exists and contributes to park management, it should be supplied. This is in the spirit of reciprocity that is the core of any statistical program. As people (park staff or national offices) learn they can rely on these data, the applications will spread. As applications spread the importance of accuracy at all levels will become more apparent. At Level IV there will be a public use reporting program manager who will have to address such needs and fulfill the general reporting requirements as well. Such a program manager will be responsible for quality control (check detail, reporting, record keeping, equipment installation and operation, etc.) and act as a consultant to the needs of other staff (scheduling patrols and pickup, placement and design of signage, monitoring areas showing new signs of visitor impact, etc.). A regular cycle of brief visitor surveys is conducted to update factors used in reporting and serve other staff needs.

2.5.1 WHAT IS REPORTED AT LEVEL IV

A DEVELOPED program, such as Level IV, makes cost-effective use of automatic counters to reduce error and to relieve staff of tedious duties. Limited funding may mean only one counter can be added at a time. In the Mangrove Protected Area we would start by adding a counter at the entrance gates (split duty at the NW gate for half of the month and SE gate for the other half). Next we would add an optical sensor to count visitors at the visitor center.

These guidelines include an implicit hierarchy of data. While the INTERMEDIATE Level III involved calculations made from limited survey data and manual counts existing from the INITIAL program, the DEVELOPED Level IV involves calculations made from automated counts and survey data. While what is reported remains essentially the same, accuracy and reliability of data are improved and burdens on staff are greatly reduced. What is reported is close to actual park use although survey data will always be needed for adjustments (visits, entries, and exclusions), and calculations (size of group and length of

FIGURE 2: MANGROVE PROTECTED AREA

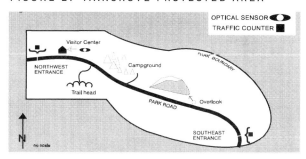

stay). As park staff become accustomed to dealing with accurate data, their needs and concerns will turn more toward preventive monitoring of incidental or emergent use (Table 5).

2.5.2 SHORTCOMINGS OF LEVEL IV

The major remaining shortcoming of public use reporting at the DEVELOPED level is the clerical job of collecting the different counts, making whatever calculations remain to be made and filing the records. Even though at least one person is assigned to consolidate this work, that person will probably get help from others who collect campground registration forms and read traffic counters. To the extent that monthly records are cumulative, errors will accumulate from month to month. Short of careful, independent review, there is no known way to get records to correct themselves.

▶ Counting of registration forms and calculation of items from separate records is error-prone.

A final step is to automate public use data collection and reporting. Until this system is automated, it will still be prone to clerical and record keeping errors. While automation cannot eliminate all errors, it can eliminate many and leave the remainder easier to identify and correct.

2.5.3 BENEFITS OF LEVEL IV

There are many benefits of a DEVELOPED, Level IV program. The benefits of this level include all of the uses covered above, including information for maintenance operations, visitor services and protection, natural resource protection, and

TABLE 5: WHAT IS REPORTED AT LEVEL IV (DEVELOPED PUBLIC USE REPORTING PROGRAM)

		REPORTED	METHOD
Visits		YES	AC
	Corrected for Counter Error?	YES	
	Adjusted for Excluded Use?	YES	Survey
	Adjusted for Entries?	YES	Survey
Visitor Hours		YES	Survey
Entries		YES	Survey
Visitor Nights		YES	MC & Survey
Visitor Night Hours		YES	Survey Average
Entry Night Hours		YES	Survey

MC = Manual Count   AC = Automated Count   ES = Estimate (partial count)   AD = Adjustment
CS = Constant   CV = Conversion   CC = Calculation   AP = Approximation

general management. Level IV has the depth and accuracy that stimulates more confidence in its use.

2.6 LEVEL V: ADVANCED PUBLIC USE REPORTING PROGRAM

The purpose of an ADVANCED, Level V, program is still resource protection, visitor safety and other applications described earlier. In addition, at this level the program becomes a showcase and center for teaching, research and problem solving for parks in the region at large. Not every park within a group of parks needs to have an ADVANCED public use reporting program. However, parks or protected areas with high volumes of use, extensive development or planned development, or critical and threatened resource conditions would be well served by the precision, depth, and usefulness that is associated with an ADVANCED program.

Attributes of Level V include trained staff dedicated to the program, the use of computers, enhanced graphic and statistical presentations of data, additional detail for all park operating departments beyond those that have already been discussed. At this stage visitor surveys are conducted quarterly consisting of policy and issue specific items as well as statistical and research oriented questions. Other studies might include data about transportation, evaluation, activity, perception, etc. At this stage the applications of data become especially important, not just to the park itself but to the entire system of parks it represents. The park use data can confidently be used for regional economic evaluation. Data on the economic impact of park use and the kinds of specific expenditures people make are usually highly valued by local businesses and political leaders.

As part of the emergence of the park as a learning center, formal relationships with nearby university faculty and students bring together the energy of youth, guidance of their academic leaders and help solve some of the problems of resource managers. As a summary of program development, the Table 6 is offered.

Along with Table 6, the following caveat is offered. The amounts of staff, time and funding do not necessarily make the difference between a program of one level or another. They do not account for the difference between data which are either superficial and unreliable on one hand or completely sufficient to management's needs on the other. Even though our example is presented as a series of progressions from one level to another, this is not necessarily the case. The complicating factor is the need for data. For example, a historic structure with a single entrance and no overnight use could have a very simple counting program to which it would be hard to assign a level.

2.7 HOW FAR TO GO?

Throughout the progression of steps toward a comprehensive program of public use reporting, field staff and management personnel need to test the data for applicability to the needs of management. Parks should make the decision to improve data collection when they see the need to improve their own actions to protect the area and to serve the public.

The development of a program must be coordinated with all park staff whether directly involved in the current program or not. It is likely that changes will affect everyone in the park. Early sensitization is part of the basic preventative function of monitoring public use. It is suggested that some rotation of counting effort and equipment be integrated into the evolving program from the beginning. To the extent that the park is a dynamically changing place, the occurrence of and provision for change in public use and associated development will also change.

Future park professionals might handle change differently. An alternative is the provision of multiple and temporary access points allowing for dispersion of demand and enabling the reversal of development even as we have seen demand abate from time to time. Further changes in synthetic materials and construction technology may lead to additional options for those who look for them.

The First Law of Crisis Management states: if one labors exclusively to solve the problem of the impending, however well one accomplishes the needs of the moment, one is predestined to repeat the mistakes of the past. If managers are to protect the resource, they must step back and take a longer view. A way to do that is to include flexibility in the statistical program (and every other major program). It is important to constantly evaluate the data collection system and the products from the data analysis. A long-term view and careful evaluation of the data collection procedures will lead to continual improvement in the accuracy of the data and the usefulness of the data.

2.8 HOW THE GUIDELINES WORK

The following chapters contain sections that deal with various topics such as counting instruments and visitor surveys. Few areas will contain all of the information needed or available.

TABLE 6: LEVELS OF PROGRAM DEVELOPMENT

LEVEL	STAFF	TIME	FUNDING
Initial	1 (other duties as assigned)	(as time permits)	None
Basic	1 (other duties as assigned)	10% allocated	Nominal
Intermediate	2 (other duties as assigned)	25% allocated	Same as small operating department
Developed	1 (dedicated to program)	100%	Same as any operating department
Advanced	2+ (dedicated to program)	100%	Enhanced

Each section is intended to provide users with a basic understanding of the subject. Sections will be revised and replaced over time to create documentation which is evolutionary along the lines of technological developments and user experience and comment.

Taita Hills Safari Lodge, Kenya

Globally, the number of private ecotourism reserves has increased dramatically in recent years. For public policy reasons, it is important to tabulate the use levels of both public and private parks.

CHAPTER 3

STATISTICS – CONTINUOUS COUNTING SYSTEMS

3.0 INTRODUCTION

Chapter 3 covers the continuous measurement or estimation of public use for a park or protected area. Such counts are made monthly and summarized annually or as needed. Data from individual reporting areas around the world can be pooled as an indicator of movement on the path of planetary understanding.

3.1 MEASUREMENT OPTIONS

Park use can be measured by a variety of methods. Indeed, a mixture of methods is the recommended solution for most areas. Assuming widespread shortage of staff and hard currency, some mixture of methods will be the most cost-effective path for parks to follow for some time. If the standard definitions given above are followed, parks using entirely different methods can produce data which are compatible and comparable.

The following discussion covers three basic ways to count, by instruments, from administrative records, and by making simple calculations. The public use reporting system selected by the protected area manager will consist of that combination of methods which can be reliably performed at the moment. Many parks will not be able to measure all use nor will future use be the same as it is now. The reporting system will change and get better. The resulting data will also get better and find their way into decisions and issues that now are lacking.

3.2 INSTRUMENTATION

There are a variety of technologies which produce instruments that automatically detect and record objects. The instruments react to mass, temperature, or motion made by horses, people, cars, snowmobiles, boats, etc. For the purchase price of one counter, a park or protected area can automatically measure traffic at a point on a road or trail. For the cost of about five of these counters a resource manager can equip the area with a rotating schedule of partial counting at points on 15 to 25 road or trails (depending on the frequency of relocating counters).

With any instrument using small amounts of electricity, attention needs to be given to the possibility of electrical interference (both electromagnetic and radio interference) from automobile ignitions, radios, etc. Technical specifications given by manufacturers are averages and may not take into account circumstantial impediments or improvements such as better radio frequency range possible with alternative antenna design or positioning arrangements.

In addition, hardware is not foolproof. Each installation requires some field trials before measurements can be taken for the record. All counting assemblies should be independently verified. Raw data from counters will usually have to be adjusted to some extent. Most equipment, for example, is insensitive to parallel traffic where two or more objects intersect a sensor (possibly in opposite directions) at the same time and are measured as one.

Instrument assemblies may include any combination of sensors (separate or combined emitter and receiver), cables or transmitters and recorders and associated power supplies. When considering any assembly, remember that the power supply that has to be changed most often dictates the maintenance of the entire assembly. A passive infrared emitter may run for months on a small battery. However, if the emitter is coupled with a power hungry receiver (as with active infrared) which transmits a signal to a remote recorder, it is the short life of the receiver/transmitter that counts most. With the rapid decrease in size and increase in the power of portable computers, it is now feasible to have data recorders download directly into computer data bases. Some parks use solar cells attached to batteries to power remote sensors, as well as their associated computers and transmitters.

Most of the technology has been developed for the manufacturing environment, for high level security, for assembly-line and robotics control where human safeguard and fail-safe accuracy are of concern. Most instruments are available in structurally tough, corrosion resistant, non-conducting thermoplastic material.

3.3 CONTACT SENSORS

Contact sensors include any device which comes into close or direct contact with the activity being measured: magnetic detectors in the shape of pads, mats, or cables, and seismic (vibration) detectors in the shape of spikes, mats, structural clamps, and other physically activated detectors.

3.4 MAGNETIC DETECTORS

Magnetic detectors activate counters when ferromagnetic metals (bicycles to automobiles) pass over and change the ambient magnetic field of the earth or an artificial field created by a charged cable. The most common type of magnetic sensor has been the electrically charged cable buried in the road surface. More recently magnetic sensors also come in the shape of small pads (as small as 8 square inches or 20 sq. cm.) which are spiked onto the road surface. The pads are easy to install, hard to see, and cheap to replace. Some may be read directly from small LED (light-emitting diode) displays while others require cable connections to portable computers.

3.5 ADVANTAGES OF MAGNETIC DETECTORS

There are advantages with the use of magnetic detectors. When magnetic counters are used with buried cable, they are vandal-proof, wear resistant and close to indestructible. Buried cable is inexpensive. Magnetic counters can be rotated between numerous locations (either systematically or according to a random sampling plan). The counts are then expanded mathematically to represent the entire reporting period. For example, if a counter is rotated between two locations for equal periods, the counts are doubled to represent the entire period.

3.6 DISADVANTAGES OF MAGNETIC DETECTORS

There are disadvantages to the use of magnetic detectors. The applications are primarily for vehicular traffic (special hardware is available for bicycle paths). Installation is labor intensive, and therefore costly. Installation includes time for careful adjustments for delay to prevent double counting of lengthy vehicles, slow-moving vehicles and vehicles with towed equipment. Readjustment of sensitivity levels may be needed for traffic with highly variable rates. The equipment requires battery replacement at intervals.

REFERENCES
National Park Service. 1988. A Guide for the Installation of Loop Detectors for Traffic Counting Purposes. Denver Service Center, National Park Service, Department of the Interior, United States of America.

United States Forest Service. 1983. Inductive Loops: Their Design, Installation and Maintenance for Road Traffic Surveillance. Equipment Development Center, Forest Service, Department of Agriculture, Missoula, Montana, No. 7700-9.

The United States Forest Service Equipment Development Center has reviewed a variety of pedestrian and traffic measurement instruments. For a publication on the findings see U.S. Forest Service, Technology Development Program, April 1994, Publication 2E22A89, Recreation, Missoula, Montana 59801, United States. U.S. Government Printing Office publication 1994-589-244/800019.

3.7 SEISMIC DETECTORS

Seismic sensors are activated by direct pressure or vibrations from physical disturbance. They come in the shape of floor or surface mats, spikes driven into asphalt surfaced roadways, tubes or canisters buried in the ground along trails or clamped onto rigid structures subject to vibration during use. When buried, these sensors and their antennas are undetectable as long as they are not exposed by trail wear or erosion. Seismic sensors are adjustable for both sensitivity and reset interval (delay). Some seismic sensors can detect activity as far as three meters away (10 feet). As traffic passes within an area a signal is transmitted to a receiver. Receivers can be located as far as 90 meters (100 yards) away from the sensor. Some equipment is modulated (tone-coded) to reduce interference from other sources. The receiver can be connected to a variety of devices including counters, cameras, and video equipment. Temporary connections to visual monitors would enable users to determine factors needed to adjust counts to visitors at different sensitivity settings.

3.8 ADVANTAGES OF SEISMIC DETECTORS

There are advantages to the use of seismic detectors. They can be adjusted to detect either vehicular or pedestrian traffic. If the soil and vegetation cover are restored to original condition, seismic detectors cannot be seen by park visitors. Buried sensors are resistant to weather conditions and remain operational for years. Some models broadcast counts to receivers located away from the sensor itself (look for pulsed or tone-coded features to avoid radio frequency interference). Some models are designed for use with photographic or video equipment.

3.9 DISADVANTAGES OF SEISMIC DETECTORS

There are disadvantages to the use of seismic detectors for the counting of visitor use. Seismic detector installations buried in the ground can be exposed over time by soil erosion or flotation in certain soil conditions. Seismic detectors are inappropriate for some applications such as caves or archeological sites were digging may be inappropriate. The location of the cable connectors to the buried sensors must be mapped for removal later. The odds are high that the map will lose itself as personnel change over the long life of the sensors. It is very important that all data collection procedures be thoroughly documented. Delay and sensitivity testing are important for proper adjustment. Average settings may not be appropriate for all rates of traffic flow. Operation will vary according to soil conditions. These instruments are relatively insensitive to clustered traffic. The distinction between human and wildlife may be difficult to make. Batteries are used in both sensor and receiver or counter and battery life is limited to several months. Some models are inappropriate for applications where traffic stops on the sensor.

Alligator and Road Counter, Jean Lafitte National
Historical Park and Reserve, USA

Traffic counters on roads sometimes record
travel other than vehicles.

3.10 OPTICAL SENSORS

Light waves vary in frequency across a range or
spectrum with invisible X-rays at one end and
invisible "far infrared" at the other. Visible sunlight
has a frequency in the middle of the light
spectrum. Different kinds of light have different
properties. The infrared band remains effective
under a variety of lighting conditions such as rain,
snow, fog or blowing dust which would obscure
other sources of light. This makes infrared a good
detector for the outdoor applications needed by
resource managers.

Three modes of infrared sensing are most
common. The opposed mode (also called active
infrared or beam-break) is where an object (up to
350 feet or 107 meters away) passes between an
emitter and its receiver, breaks the beam and
registers a count on a recorder. In the retro-
reflexive mode (another kind of active infrared)
the emitter also contains the receiver which

registers a count when an object breaks a signal
from a reflector (up to 225 feet or 70 meters
distant).

Some active infrared emitters make use of digital
modulated light (emissions which switch on and
off at precise frequencies that receivers are tuned
to pick up). Modulated sensors are easier to align,
use less power and respond only to light of a
specific frequency. Modulated signals are also a
part of the detection function of emitters.
Receivers count the return signal and register a
count only if the signal is blocked for that amount
of time determined to be attributable to traffic. The
receiver then counts more signals waiting for the
path to clear before it resets.

In the diffuse mode (or passive infrared) there is
no separate reflector other than the object itself
which will reflect (up to 100 feet or 30 meters)
some signal back to the emitter/receiver. In some
instances equipment can be installed in pairs to

double the effective range. Many instruments include audio/visual indicators that make alignment easy and also tell when the signal strength is low.

Optical sensors also use visible light from incandescent bulbs. Such light has generally greater intensity and range but visibility makes it prone to vandalism. Sensors are also sensitive to unintended light from nearby sources and reflections (proxing). Polarizing filters cut down the field of vision of the visible light and the chances that it will react to reflections or be observed by anyone not looking directly at the source. Unfortunately, such filters cut down the optical intensity of the beam.

Optical instrumentation performance specifications should be carefully studied relative to each proposed installation. Emitter signal strength (called excess gain) diminishes with distance and clarity of the operating environment. Manufacturers provide guides suggesting the limits of each model regarding conditions, distance, and required signal strength. Infrared beam patterns vary according to the type of emitter in use. Some will remain fairly focused at some distance requiring careful alignment, especially visible lasers which have great range.

Some attention to the detail of installation is required. If optics are mounted at waist level to count vehicles, as is the standard for pedestrian counting, an optical traffic counter will probably count passenger heads through auto windows (mounting on the vertical diagonal is recommended). Similarly, optical counters should not be located perpendicular to trails so they can count individuals walking abreast (unless the trail is very narrow). Care should be given to the direction of sunrise and sunset to avoid alignment of the "eye" directly with the sun which will saturate any kind of optical sensor if not burn it out entirely.

The lenses used in all of this equipment can vary and lens design (image enlargement) can amplify the effective range of emitters but with corresponding limitations due to atmospheric clutter. (See O'Rourke, 1994 for a comparative study of eight different optical systems.)

A range of instruments and manufacturers using this technology is available. Several instruments have been specifically designed for outdoor applications in regard to size, demand on batteries, concealment, and range.

3.11 ADVANTAGES OF OPTICAL SENSORS

Optical sensors have some advantages. Optical sensor technology is no longer limited to low light interior spaces. Some optical sensors can cover a wide distance such as across a body of water or landing strip (up to 700 feet or 215 meters for visible laser beams). Used in pairs, ranges can double what is shown in specifications. The devices provide high levels of accuracy at low cost. Most optical sensor assemblies have an effective operational range of -35 to 50 C (-30 to 120 F) with lithium batteries. Such batteries cost

Hikers in Yoho National Park, Canada
There are many technologies available for the automatic recording of visitor use on trails.

less than US $10 per year for batteries and can be purchased for about US $200. Several kinds of applicable optical sensors are tough and need little attention for long periods. Infrared can be used to measure any heat emitting source including bicycle and horseback riders, hikers, and vehicles. They will not react to falling leaves, snow, trailers towed by cars, or hikers swinging walking sticks. Instrument sensitivity in the form of reset interval can be adjusted to avoid duplicate counting expected from certain activity (horse, bicycle and canoe traffic).

This technology has yet to be fully explored for its potential benefits. Optical sensors are useful in areas where an entrance may involve an irregular configuration, such as circular entrances in historic buildings and outdoor spaces involving concave terrain.

3.12 DISADVANTAGES OF OPTICAL SENSORS

While robust in the presence of atmospheric clutter, optical sensors are prone to suffer from frost on lenses and dirt accumulation. The "eye" can be protected by recessing it away from the elements or by manual cleaning at intervals. While laser diode emitters have the longest range, alignment becomes more critical. Fractional offsets become spans of misalignment when projected into the distance. Alignment can also be disturbed by vibrations or platform shifting due to humidity or temperature variations. O'Rourke (1994) reported different sensitivities to clothing with active infra-red tending to misread light clothing and passive infra-red tending to misread dark clothing. While light, small, inexpensive and easy to install, diffuse or passive infrared equipment provides less range and accuracy due to the higher sensitivity levels needed for weak return signals. That makes them error-prone due to variations in reflectivity, contrast, ambient light and thermal conditions.

Wide detection zones characteristic of passive infra-red are not always an advantage. The longer the "target" remains in the detection zone, the longer will be the delay before the instrument can reset (sometimes up to 3 to 4 seconds). This characteristic can be offset by installations along difficult portions of a trail. These may be prone to vandalism, especially where visible light and reflectors of active infra-red are involved. Nonlinear applications involving mirrors can expect a 30% loss of signal at each point of reflection which will substantially reduce effective range. Any application involving polarization will lose about 50% of signal.

REFERENCES

Banner Engineering Corp. 1993. Handbook of Photoelectric Sensing. Banner Engineering Corp., Minneapolis, Minnesota, United States of America.

O'Rourke, D. 1994. Trail Traffic Counters for Forest Service Trail Monitoring. United States Forest Service, Technology Development Program, Publication 2E22A89, Recreation, Missoula, Montana 59801. U.S. Government Printing Office publication 1994-589-244/800019. U.S. Forest Service, Technology Development Center, Building 1, Fort Missoula, Missoula, Montana 59801. United States of America.

3.13 OTHER TECHNOLOGY

The application of technology to the task of resource monitoring has yet to be fully developed. The use of fiber-optical cable, for example, means optical sensors can be far removed from what they measure with little loss of signal. The limits of optical, sonic and magnetic sensing have yet to be fully tested in submerged environments in rivers and lakes where use is often unmeasured.

Microwave detectors are primarily designed for use along automobile roadways in conjunction with doorway and traffic control systems (activation of doors and traffic lights). Microwave emitter/receivers detect motion (above 3 km per hour) of any mass out to a maximum range of about 107 meters (350 feet). At that distance the cone of sensitivity covers about 11 meters across

(36 feet). The advantage of microwave is its relatively broad area of sensitivity (up to 30 x 120 feet or 9 X 36.6 meters) can sense direction of travel without the use of turnstiles or constrictive zones.

The use of ultrasonic detectors is primarily in conjunction with traffic controller applications such as presence sensing to prevent gates or doors from closing on objects. Ultrasound emitters are used to produce an inaudible signal (above 20 kHz) which reflects or "echos" off of solid objects at relatively short distances (15 meters or less). The advantage of ultrasound is less sensitivity to the surface condition of the sensed object than optical emissions which tend to react differently to color and light reflectivity. That advantage does not include sound reflectivity. Sound absorbing surfaces are not good targets for ultrasound which limits their uses for trail applications (human/wildlife sensing). Ultrasound can measure distances from the reflected object which is an advantage not found in other traffic sensors. Ultrasound is among the more costly technologies.

Turnstiles and hand counters will remain appropriate technology for measuring public use for a long time. Turnstiles can be installed at any place where pedestrian traffic is funneled through a narrow space. People are counted individually as they pass through a rotating gate. A portion of the gate rotation is recorded by a simple mechanical counter. Hand counters are useful in situations when staff can devote most of their attention to group turnover such as in a theater, amphitheater, or equivalent presentation. As a source of continuous recording by an individual tasked with other responsibilities, data compiled by hand counters is error prone.

Pneumatic hoses are used where vehicles may make an impact and activate an air pressure sensitive counter. Pneumatic counters are sensitive to traffic from 1 kilometer per hour or higher. In hot climates rubber hoses will be sunk into asphalt. Hoses are also prone to deterioration in direct sun. Installations across dirt or loose rock should be reinforced to prevent hoses from becoming buried. Installation should avoid curves which will involve excessive wear and miscounting. Hoses require frequent examination for tears which allow air out and moisture in, causing the system to fail. Records of the installation of new hoses will guide the frequency of inspection required as hoses age. Ideally they should be located near entrance stations, congested areas or stop signs where the chance of vandalism is reduced.

Photographic sampling is an important extension of the basic measurement task. Surveillance cameras are useful for remote sensing of large areas (100 meters plus). They can be installed to be activated randomly or at regular intervals for areas where activity is low or unknown. Time lapse photography can be used to sample public use across broad fields of view. While some cameras come with intervalometers which activate the shutter at set intervals, intervalometers can be purchased separately. A small frame (e.g., 8 mm) motion picture camera activated by an appropriate sensor (e.g., passive infra-red) would be able to count thousands of visitors before replacement, as well as differentiate between people and wildlife. Such an application would yield both a human and animal census. Visual media, of course, sort out what is counted when wildlife and human populations intermix.

3.14 REMOTES — TRANSCEIVERS, RECORDERS, FIBER OPTIC CABLES

Emitter, receiver, transmitter, recorder associated cabling and power supplies may be in one package from one manufacturer, packaged separately, or packaged in some combination. The possibilities for combination include multi-optic cable feeds to video cameras which detect hot-spots replacing the tedious function of the fire watch.

A device called a transceiver can be used to extend the range of measurement equipment to recorders by hundreds of kilometers (within range of overflying park aircraft). At least one manufacturer has a small transceiver that contains data memory, a real time clock, receiver, transmitter and power supply. The transceiver can store data, listen for transmission instructions, and broadcast data on demand as far as a mile away (or up). Such a transceiver could upload weather and surface resource conditions including wind velocity, wind direction, humidity, temperature, soil conditions, or any other measurable quality of the environment needed by park managers.

Fiber optic cables made of glass can be used to extend the reach of optical sensors. These cables are rugged and flexible. Applications include caves and other remote environments where the sensor, power pack and recorder assembly needs to be more conveniently located than the area where sensing is actually taking place.

3.15 SECONDARY RECORDS

Counting handouts at entrance stations is an efficient and reasonably accurate method of estimating visitors. Since "counts" are made by comparing the end volume with the beginning volume, park staff are free to engage visitors as needed without losing track. Asking staff to make counts with a hand counter while engaging in material distribution should be avoided. The obvious distractions for the staff leads to errors in counting.

There are often existing local activities which count visitors independent of the park or protected area itself. Railway stations, marine landings, bus operators, and airports may have their own reasons to keep track of nearby traffic. While such data may include non-park activity, there may be ways to make adjustments that will give an indication of the portion which has the park or protected area as its destination. Local

accommodations may be used as jump-off points for visitors and those occupancy statistics could be used. While it would be cost effective to have others collect statistics on behalf of the park, consideration must be given to the limitations which bear on such numbers. There may be a proprietary interest in withholding such data from competitors. Government regulations covering taxation and immigrations may create bias or other constraints. Secondary records may be poorly kept or kept in ways which are too time consuming to recover compared to the simple monthly reading of automated instruments.

3.16 VISITOR REGISTERS

A simple, but effective and useful way to collect attendance data is through the register. A register is simply a form on which people record their trip to the park. In addition to registration, parks often encourage people to place a colored pin on their hometown on a world map (the maps are changed periodically). People are naturally curious to see if they are the only ones to visit or if there are others from home. If a park has brochures to give out, it can be done along with a request to register. Most people will respond to the trade of a name and address for a brochure.

A register is easy to design and make. Some registers are simply titled lines on a page covering date of visit, hometown, number in group, and visitor comments. Such registers are commonly presented on a large, attractive binder displayed on a podium at a visitor center entrance. Registers are a way of communicating a "welcome" to the park.

A register can also be in the form of a card with date, name, address, and other information needed by the park. Cards can be passed out wherever people are to be found (overlooks, visitor centers, entrances, program presentations). If cards are methodically collected, they can be invaluable. They account for visitation volume, tell something about the visitor, and give visitors an opportunity to communicate back to the park (the "comments" part). If an effort is made to have all visitors register, the accuracy of estimated visitation counting can be as good as counting by instruments. Registration is usually easier and always cheaper than counting by instrument considering the trials of instrument calibration, breakdown, maintenance, and regular data recording. Registers, especially cards, can be designed to include such diverse information as sites visited, activities, expenditures, etc.

One should be cautious not to ask for more information than can be reasonably expected when registration is voluntary. There are, of course, conditions where registration is not voluntary; usually for reasons which are in the interests of public welfare or resource protection. Where registration is not voluntary, the purpose of registration should be conspicuously displayed to the park visitors to encourage submission of registration information. Keeping track of people is an important resource management function that most people understand. Some kind of traffic control is usually needed to avoid bunching up on resources such as rivers, trails, caves, etc. It is appropriate to remind people if they are entering a wild area because search and rescue is an expensive and occasionally tragic event. Asking people to record their visit plans is a way to capture their attention and possibly help them avoid needing help. However, if help is required, having the key information on the visitor will be of critical assistance. In environments which pose periodic hazards (snake bites, slippery surfaces, hypothermia, etc.), the need for registration is also an appropriate time to hand out literature on safe practices.

Registers are also useful for general management and planning purposes. Some people will develop a lingering interest in the park and its future. If there are management questions to which the park wants a viewpoint, the registration of interest is a good way to gather address data for newsletters. (Be careful, on the other hand, not to promise what cannot be delivered.)

In cases where registration is not required of all visitors, verification of register use can be accomplished by simply asking (at regular intervals) a certain number of people exiting the park if they registered anywhere in the park during their visit. Of course, periodical checks of registration against door counts (assuming there is a way of measuring foot traffic) can give an indication of registration frequency among the public. That leaves open the question of how many park visitors use the facility where registration occurs.

If a park decides to use registration, a mixed strategy can work well, e.g., using guest registers in combination with cards for certain activities or during a sample of the visitor season. Records from entrance fees, wilderness permits, trail head and campground registers can fill in the gaps.

©Parks Canada/P.S.T. Jacques

Park Visitors and Park Staff at Forillon National Park, Canada

Park visitor service personnel are often very busy with the provision of information and advice to park visitors. Often they are too occupied to be able to accurately count park visitor use by casual observation.

Prince Edward Island National Park Campground Program, Canada
Interpretive programs keep records of attendance.

Care should be taken not to use sources which will result in duplication of counts, e.g., visitors who register at visitor centers, at campgrounds, and also at trail heads. Special attention needs to be given to the sources used. Fees paid for campground use, for example, are a good source if the fee is per person per night or if party size is recorded along with fee payment. Entrance fees, on the other hand, might not be a good source if the fee is for unlimited entrancing over a period of time. Such complexities as these are what drive parks to implement instrument counting systems.

Registers should be closed out at intervals, the data summarized in a report and the originals discarded. Making use of register data can be time consuming. But considering the costs of instrumentation, they remain an attractive and reasonable alternative for small to moderate statistical systems or as a way to start a statistical program while waiting for funds for instrumentation and installation.

3.17 OBSERVATIONS

The use of informal observation as the basis for collecting data is common and completely appropriate for statistics used for public relations purposes. To the extent that managers have real, immediate, and practical uses for data, they can only rely on formal observations, i.e., observations made according to strict rules of record keeping.

If park staff are stationed at places where occasional visitation occurs and if they are required to record each instance of visitation, the cumulation of observation records can be considered factual. If park staff are asked to recall their observations at a later time for a particular interval of time, the recollection of events is not factual nor appropriate for use of any consequence.

If park staff are provided with a sampling plan for making observed counts of consistently identified objects (which could be persons, occupants of a campsite, vehicles, etc.) at defined areas and specified points of observation, such data can be considered to be factual. Any methodical enumeration such as daily counts at a certain hour would be considered factual. Areas should be precisely defined so counts taken by more than one observer will have some consistency.

Circumstances, unfortunately, tend to corrupt observations despite the best intentions of observers. Questions from visitors, emergency situations, rule violations, illness, or absenteeism and all kinds of human error can confound observations. Any need to use observations should be a primary assignment for the observer rather than one of several duties while on patrol.

The use of hand counters is strongly advised. If observers are free from distraction, several hand counters can be combined for multiple counts, e.g., number of people on shore versus off shore, horseback riders versus hikers. Multiple counting can become complicated, such as for campground managers who want to know male, female, adults, children, pets, bag-tent-trailer (vehicle), flotation equipment, etc. Tally sheets can ease this headache. Nevertheless, remember that observations are error prone and detailed observations are more so!

Other than the distinctions between gender and adult or child, socio-demographic characteristics cannot be observed. Generally, group membership cannot be observed. There is also difficulty in observing activity. Activities can change from moment to moment, with weather conditions, or based on what other people in the visiting group are doing.

3.18 CALCULATIONS, COUNTER ROTATION, PARTIAL COUNTS

The accuracy of direct counting declines as the number of traffic counters needed to cover an area increases. As the number of traffic counters increases, so do equipment failures, vandalism, and errors of record-keeping.

If the park has personnel in the field, there is a way to cover large areas without involving scores

of instruments and keeping a warehouse of batteries. Counters can be rotated between sensors according to a plan for sampling various areas of the park. The resulting partial counts can be expanded to represent the entire area. However, the design of such a data collection procedure will be complex and must be very carefully designed and carried out.

3.19 COLLECTION SYSTEM DESIGN

Unfortunately, few parks have physical layouts which involve a single entrance/exit point which can be automatically measured. Most parks need to draw from a variety of measurement techniques and apply them to a variety of locations ranging from entrances, landing points, watering holes, campgrounds, or other gathering spots.

The design of a collection system has a range of compromises. Accuracy is good but complexity, which increases with accuracy, is bad. Completeness is good, but high cost and effort which increase with completeness, is bad. Cheap and easy systems are good, but staff forgetfulness and indifference, which increase with minimal priority and effort, is bad.

Resource management needs will dictate the design of any system. If, for example, management needs to know the difference between heavy traffic (horses, mountain bikes, snowmobiles) and light traffic (cross-country skiing, hiking), it can be done. Dual sensors, seismic for heavy traffic and infra-red for all traffic, would provide the necessary data.

Finally, the design of a collection system should involve some experimentation. Experimentation will help identify when direct counts are needed and when approximations, constants, or estimates will do. To the extent that seasonal changes and shifting markets of visitors are involved, the collection system may involve several configurations at different times.

At Buffalo National River Park in the USA, a passive infra-red system is used to measure boats going downstream. The need for this data is in the park river management plan. The assembly has been installed with consideration of periodic flood levels and at such a point that it detects a relatively fast moving section where boaters are more likely to be in single file. Fast-moving channels are preferred because of the minimum three-second delay between counts. Verification of the system indicates an error of about 2% due to traffic moving slowly or across the channel and remaining in the beam long enough to be counted again.

Some parks are composed of several units, geographically separated from each other. An example of such a situation is the Richmond National Battlefield Park in the USA. This park is typical of any multi-unit park (a park with a discontinuous boundary). The collection of accurate, and therefore useful, data from such sites requires a sophisticated system. Use of each unit is measured by contact counters (pneumatic and inductive loops), adjusted for the traffic pattern (one or two way), adjusted for visits (compared to visits and entries), non-reportable traffic, and persons per vehicle multiplier. The subtotal for all areas is added and multiplied by a factor which represents the amount of multi-unit visitation and the product is the grand total for the period. All the factors used in the calculation are derived from a multi-seasonal visitor survey using a randomly selected sampling scattered throughout each month. Such surveys are updated at intervals of about three years.

3.20 CONVERTING INSTRUMENT MEASUREMENTS TO REPORTABLE DATA

It is often necessary to convert readings from instruments to numbers which indicate public use. Such conversions may involve factors which may enlarge counts (such as persons per vehicle greater than 1.0) or factors which may reduce counts (such as a visit less than 1.0 to account for non reportable use). The determination of Persons-Per-Vehicle (PPV) and re-entry Length-Of-Stay (LOS), Visits or Entries, exit-re-entry or other factors that may be needed are covered in the following chapter on visitor studies.

3.21 AUTOMATION

Any statistical program involves activities that are tedious and require attention to detail including the collection and recording of data from several locations, conversion of data to reportable statistics, correction of erroneous entries, archiving and recovery of data for various applications. At some point in the development of a public use reporting program it is necessary to acquire a computer to store and process data. Of course, there are many other reasons why

Faculty of the Griffith University School of Leisure Studies, Australia

One of the functions of the head office is to develop liaison with university faculty and departments.

computers are becoming tools that are basic to any administrative activity.

One kind of computer software that deals with data processing of the kind we have discussed is called forms management software. An example is included in Chapter 6 called "EZ Forms Database." This program allows a form for entering data to be tailor-made according to the needs of a user. The forms can be mathematically related to each other so that cumulative information can automatically be carried from one form to another. The data entered become part of a relational database. Later data can be recovered in whatever order or format is desired. The applications of forms management software are not limited to public use data. An indirect benefit of the development of a methodical public use reporting program is those skills and abilities that will benefit every other area of park management from basic administration to resource management itself.

3.22 CENTRAL OFFICE FUNCTIONS

The public use reporting function at central offices provides a variety of essential services including the prescription of reporting intervals, the preparation of useful feedback to parks, and the definition and regulation of standards. In the central office, a few individuals with experience in program development, technology and automation can provide invaluable assistance. Central offices can also provide depot level maintenance, procurement and inventory support.

Many park agencies develop a visitor management or tourism management office in the head office or at some other central location. One key task of the central office is to develop agency procedures, then to implement the procedures and monitor compliance. An example of a form, developed by Parks Canada for each of its field units, to track the visitor attendance methodology in each park in a system is found in Appendix 2.

The central office can keep track of the suppliers of specialized equipment, of software and of computer technology. System wide surveys are best designed in a central locale, by specially trained staff, and then administered in the field. Sophisticated survey design, statistical analysis and report production is usually a central office role. It important for the head office to keep track of trends in visitor management and tourism analyses. Forming partnerships with universities expert in tourism and leisure management is an important function of the central office.

The central office can serve as a reviewer and auditor of field data. Standardization of the data collection procedures and checking of the data for validity is best done by those with specialized training. The central office can play a pivotal role in training of the field staff.

Reporting to government and to the public about use levels of a park system is a critical function. When the central office is sure that the data is accurate and acceptable, it has the role to provide this data to the appropriate people and institutions. The application of the data into park management, into regional tourism plans and into international policy development can be a vital role of the central office.

3.23 REPORTING INTERVALS

Park managers' most common need for data is at monthly intervals. Therefore, reports are put together monthly. However, the frequency of recording counts is another matter. If counts come from automatic counters, they can be read as needed (monthly). If counts come from manual counters or observations, they should be recorded at whatever interval they are made. Common forms for recording data should be prepared and kept as long as they may prove useful and as a check to resolve errors (usually a year).

Changes in counting procedures at the park or protected area should be enacted at the beginning of the year following the decision to change rather than as soon as changes are determined. Such a convention makes it easier to study changes among a group of parks and provides a 12-month cycle of use between changes.

Advances in computer technology and communication technology allow for shorter reporting intervals. For example, computer storage of campground registration data makes it possible for almost instantaneous delivery of data analysis reports on that data. The level of campground use, the home location of all campers and trends in use over time can all be calculated quickly and communicated widely both within the park and to a central office.

3.24 FEEDBACK

The delivery of feedback from central to field offices is necessary to establish a mutually beneficial relationship between offices. Individual parks can collect their own data but they often cannot analyze all data relevant to what is happening in their own site. Central offices can provide that service to areas that report to them. The scope and content of data reported back to parks can range from a collection of past and other park data to reports of travel conditions, airport arrivals, relative costs of motor fuel, and a wide range of useful information. That feedback or quid pro quo is what can keep a relationship between central and field offices healthy and productive. As communication continues to improve, and especially with the onset of the internet, fast and easy communication between parks and other offices becomes easier. With the internet, electronic mail and other forms of communication, parks can send their data to the central office frequently, possibly even continually. Similarly, the head office can send back analyses almost as soon as they are completed.

3.25 AUDITS

Overzealous accounts of public use can result from a range of motivations from deliberate intent to defraud to misplaced enthusiasm. Counting programs have revealed theft of park fees. Counting records have been forged to justify new construction facilities in parks. Indeed, some expensive projects have been built only to sit largely unused while the staff struggles to maintain them. A good counting program is a deterrent to corruption and a check against mismanagement. A central office audit program is a major means of quality control as well as a means of communicating to the park staff that accuracy and faithful representation of public use is important.

Quality control over public use reporting is established by regular audits of collection and reporting practices of parks. While parks are responsible for the quality and integrity of their own data for their own practical needs, some oversight is needed to deal with misplaced enthusiasm or misunderstanding of instructions for counting. Such oversight is also beneficial for maintaining continuity when staff move on to new positions as well as providing historical records in case park records are lost or destroyed.

3.26 ASSISTANCE

As the technology in use at parks becomes more involved, it is useful to have specialized skills to deal with it. The hiring of people with highly specialized skills may not be justified at an individual park, but is realistic for groups of parks. The need for specialized skills at central offices is especially evident when employee turnover at parks is high and the task of basic skills training in an agency becomes a continuous activity.

The same is true for hardware involved in public use reporting. It is usually not practical to maintain an inventory of spare parts in every park when there is only 1 or 2 automatic counters in use. A central depot for parks would be cost effective and also serve to maintain some consistency of hardware in use among parks, not to mention the possibility of savings from bulk purchasing.

Voi Store, Tsavo West National Park, Kenya

Park visitation can stimulate local involvement in tourism. Such businesses appreciate receiving appropriate levels of market information from park agencies.

CHAPTER 4

VISITOR STUDIES

4.0 INTRODUCTION

Up to this point in the guidelines we have been concerned with counts, i.e., statistics. The major concern in making counts is that they be complete (cover all of the park and all visitors) and accurate. We now turn our attention to studies. Studies are data collection efforts that can cover a broad range of characteristics of visitors, everything from their trip to the park to their evaluation of park programs. Studies are necessary to create a good statistical program for a park. Studies produce the basic correction and adjustment factors like average persons per vehicle, which are needed to read traffic counters and report park visitation.

The main difference between statistics and studies is the difference between a small amount of information about all visitors versus a large amount of information from some of the visitors. In the case of studies, we have to take special steps to be sure the visitors contacted are representative of all visitors. (This can be done with well-designed sampling methods which will be discussed in the next chapter, Chapter 5.)

4.1 GENERAL

While the next chapter (Chapter 5) is all about how to do studies, a preview of that material is useful now before we discuss the variety of studies there are to do.

First and foremost, try to find a copy of the "Q-Cat" which stands for question catalog. Last published in 1996, the Q-Cat is a list of 177 questions that have been asked repeatedly in visitor surveys. This catalog was developed by Ken Hornback and

Bill Key to promote the standardization of survey questions within the National Park Service of the United States. Each question has been carefully developed and field tested. The questions are listed by ten topic areas and by variable name. Several versions of many questions are listed. Codes for the most commonly given answers are also included. The entire catalog is available on the world wide web at the University of Waterloo. The web address is http://www.ahs.uwaterloo.ca/rec/toc.htm.

Second, even though you have access to a large number of interesting questions, studies must remain short in order not to irritate visitors by detaining them for long periods during their trip. Irritated visitors give bad information. One study cannot possibly collect all of the information you will need. If a small study is conducted each season, a large amount of information will soon be on hand. As a general rule you should be able to print all questions in your first survey on one side of a single piece of paper. If a lot of information is really needed in a hurry, try making several versions of the questionnaire and rotate the versions from location to location during the sampling period. This will probably require a full-time study coordinator.

Third, how do you best collect information from visitors? Do you collect data by interviewing people about their visit? Is it better to let people fill out forms with questions and answer choices already provided? Answers to these questions vary and opinions range widely. Our advice is to conduct a small number of interviews, gathering data about questions in which you are currently interested. Keep notes about which questions (and accompanying answers) seem to work without confusion or difficulty. Revise the initial interview form. If at all possible, gather all of the data by interview (according to a sampling plan discussed below). A good source for learning how to gather interview data can be found in Patton's (1990) book <u>Qualitative Evaluation and Interpretation</u>. However, if you must resort to handout forms as a source of data, remember there will always be questions about what voluntarily completed forms represent, regardless of the number distributed or returned.

Park Personnel and Visitors in Nahanni National Park, Canada

Park employees are often very comfortable talking to visitors. With additional training, these personnel can do a competent job of collecting specialized visitor data in a personal interview format of survey.

Fourth, study findings are generally applied to all park visitors. Therefore, studies must represent all park visitors. If a study is designed to give all visitors an equal opportunity to be included, its findings may be said to be representative and used with confidence. A large number of visitors need not be involved to produce useful results. On the other hand, no matter how many visitors are involved in a study which contacts only certain kinds of visitors (e.g., spring users of one campground), the data would not be representative nor applicable to all. See Chapter 5.1 to learn about collecting a good sample.

Finally, pay attention to details in the design of your questionnaire and give it a pretest. Certain core questions need to be covered for every visitor contact. Core items may address weather, identity of interviewer, date and location of visitor contact, number of visitors in a group, number of visitors under and over certain ages, visitor home residence, or other visitor characteristics observed by park staff. It is important to remember though, that when you ask core questions that you make sure you are really asking what you think you are asking. Often questionnaires are full of questions that do not ask what one thinks they do. This can potentially create many problems as the purpose of core questions is to address questions about the study itself, such as; Are the characteristics of the visitors roughly equivalent from study to study?

or, Are there local conditions which may unduly influence the findings? So called "filter" questions may also be needed to make sure a visitor is "qualified" by being near the end of the visit. Pick interviewers carefully, train them, and rehearse a cheerful greeting and a statement of how much the data are needed to run the park better for visitors. If handouts are used (questionnaires, maps, lists of activities, etc.), use bright colors. Simple hand drawings can enhance text. Animal figures can replace names where language is a problem. If questionnaire editing is to be done in red ink, interviewers have to be told to only use black/blue ink to fill out a form. These are the kinds of details that need to be worked out before your time as well as the public's is spent collecting data for use.

REFERENCE

Patton, M. Q. 1990. <u>Qualitative Analysis and Interpretation.</u> Newbury Park CA: Sage.

4.2 STUDIES THAT VERIFY STATISTICS FOR COUNTING

The instruments used in continuous counting systems (Chapter 3) are limited. Instruments usually cannot answer such basic questions as how many people are in the car which is counted. Campground records may not show how long visitors stay or if they have been in and out of the park more than once a day. There is no counter that can determine if people are coming to visit or just passing through. Something more is needed to resolve these and other questions for any counting program.

The most basic and essential kind of study is the one which verifies factors used in the general counting program. These surveys do not need to be conducted more frequently than once every three or four years unless there are major changes in or around the park that indicate the basic characteristics of the visitor or visit have changed.

4.2.1 PURPOSE OF QUESTIONS

The study to verify factors used in the park public use counting program is simply an extension of that statistical program. The purpose of verification studies is to both measure errors that can be present in a counting program and provide the data needed to correct for the degree of error. The rest of the studies in this chapter focus on different issues of concern to park management (economics, satisfaction, etc.).

A basic verification study will consist of questions covering seven areas.

1. It is usually necessary to separate people visiting the park (visits) from those who are passing through (park entries) and those who are not counted for statistical purposes, (e.g., concessionaire employees.)

2. In cases where visitation traffic may wander into and out of park boundaries, it may be necessary to trace the visit. Data from such a map will enable calculations to be made representing the amount of exit and re-entries associated with each entrance. Without such a correction, duplicate counting would be involved. This item is usually included even if road/boundary crossing is not a concern because the data have other applications for resource protection, traffic management, and general planning activities.

3. Some duplication of counting will be associated with the traffic of the same visitors out of and back into the park during the same day. This may be caused by a variety of developments outside the park such as communities where supplies are purchased, other scenic areas, homes of friends and relatives, etc. A specific question on this is asked because the visitor may not remember exiting and leaving as an activity covered in the previous question.

4. In cases where many visits last more than one day, the exact length of stay is needed. Length of stay information can easily be used to convert from visits to visitor hours. For example, if half of the visitors (50%) stay overnight (average stay of 42 hours) and half stay for day use only (average stay of 6 hours), the entrance of 1,000 visitors would result in 21,000 overnight hours plus 3,000 day use hours for a total of 24,000 overnight hours or (using the statistical convention of 12 hours per visitor/day for interpark comparative purposes) 2,000 visitor days. In reality, the more categories of length of stay (more than our example of day use and overnight), the greater the accuracy of subsequent calculations.

5. Visitors contacted during their visit may need to estimate their time of departure so a question about that is often included.

6. The questions about length of stay in the park (4 and 5 above) do not specifically determine if a visitor stayed in or outside of the park. A direct question is needed. If the visitor did not stay in the park overnight, a question might be

added to determine the length of stay during the days after the visitor stayed outside the park. If the visitor did stay in the park overnight, the location is usually asked in order to estimate the amount of use received by different campgrounds.

7. In the example given in 4 (above) the 1,000 visitors probably are estimated from traffic counter data which uses a persons per car factor (multiplier). If that factor were an average 2.5 persons found from asking about the number of people a visitor is traveling with, 1,000 visitors would arrive in 400 cars (1,000/2.5).

This most basic form of visitor survey is intended to verify and clarify characteristics of park use so raw counts can be corrected (for duplication) and converted to reportable statistics (covered in Chapter 1): visits, entries, visitor hours and visitor days. The exact content of a survey of this type will depend on the underlying statistical system, the actual layout of the park and activities available there, the possibilities for duplications, the adjustments or corrections that are needed to deal with any remaining deficiencies and gaps.

4.2.2 FORMAT
The content of this type of study is simple enough that one format can be used either as a handout to visitors or as a worksheet from which interviewers read questions and fill in the blanks. The following format may be used.

1. What is the main purpose of this trip?
    Visit Park__ Passing Through__ Other__

2. In the last 24 hours, where did you go and what did you do in the park?
    (Show the visitor a simplified park map; interviewer uses a short activity code list to record major activities, e.g.. hiking, camping, etc.)   Location__   Activity__

3. How many times did you enter and leave the park since this time yesterday?   __

4. When did you first enter the park on this trip? (Enter the month, day, and time of arrival to the nearest half hour.) Month___   Day___ Time___   AM/PM

5. When do you expect to leave for the last time on this trip? Month___   Day___   Time___ AM/PM

6. Did you stay overnight in the park during this trip? Yes__   No__
    If NO, how many hours a day did you spend in the park after staying overnight outside (the park)?____
    If YES, where? _____

7. How many people are traveling with you in your vehicle? __

Notice that the answers to this survey are recorded in blanks, that is, the answers are not identified and listed for the respondent. An advantage of this kind of "open" record is that it allows information to be recorded in the words of the respondent which reflects the respondent's awareness of the park environment, signage, most mentionable sites, etc. A disadvantage of "open" questions is that they may lead to numerous, ambiguous, or meaningless answers. Surveys that use "open" answer format are subsequently coded by a visitor analyst to focus on the major areas of specific interest. It is important to remember that is it more difficult to code and quantify this type of data. However, an "open" question formats can also lead to ideas and challenges of which you were previously unaware.

Statistics gathered to verify basic visitation counting programs are also used as the basis for designing more efficient studies in the future. The more that is known about how the visitor uses the park, the easier it is to design studies of minimal sample sizes which are still representative of visitors in general.

4.3 STUDIES OF THE TRIP AND VISITOR CHARACTERISTICS

Parks exist in socio-economic ecosystems that extend far beyond the park boundaries. Parks impact their surrounding communities in the way park visitors make use of those communities as they travel to the park. If a large park offers no overnight accommodations, park visitors will need a staging area at the gateways. This need translates into economic demand for goods and services which are usually beneficial to local communities.

The trip made by visitors can be traced all the way back to their home residences. The impact of the park goes that far as well. Who these park visitors are is a matter of some importance. If the park attracts people of economic means, the economic benefits along the way will be greater. If the park is a recreational oasis surrounded by undeveloped subsistence agricultural activity, the economic benefits will be less. Exotic features, beautiful scenery, recreational opportunities, historical significance, and other attributes of parks will attract different public interests and those interests become activities that have significance for the use of the park and surrounding communities.

Because a single message will not get through to everyone, park communications programs (resource interpretation, explanation of park rules, location of services, posting of hazard and safety warnings, etc.) are aimed and designed for different audiences: seniors, children, foreigners, people in groups, people on tours, locals, first-time visitors, campers, risk/adventure visitors, etc.

Information about the volume, activities, and characteristics of special populations (handicapped, families with small children, senior citizens, etc.) is a prerequisite to the cost-effective location and design of services and facilities for their use.

Transportation within the park is increasingly important. Increased car traffic in some parks mandates the use of some form of mass transportation. Such transport is expensive, and park managers need to know about visitor willingness to use and even pay for such systems. Travel data are used in forecasting park use, economic impact assessment of a park, and in transportation and planning studies. Information on "host" communities is used in park outreach communications efforts to better prepare visitors for hazards, conditions, and services found in the park. These data are also used by park concessions in gauging their business plans, planning services, and by the agency in regulating the scope of concessions' activities.

While trip and visitor characteristics studies can become involved and complicated, they can also be done simply. An illustrated questionnaire is a clever way to handle the need to collect relatively complicated trip and expenditure data at Bent's Old Fort National Historic Site, National Park Service, United States of America (Appendix 3). The questionnaire was printed on brilliant yellow paper (virtually none were found in trash cans) and handed out with a complimentary park memento (keepsake) in appreciation for (expected) cooperation. There are 12 "questions" on this fact sheet which was handed out to all park visitors during randomly selected hours for the three-month peak season (Appendix 3).

The content of this type of survey is covered in the "Q-Cat", Chapter I-III (Visitor Characteristics, Travel Characteristics, and Visit Characteristics).

4.4 STUDIES OF ECONOMIC ACTIVITY

Parks supply money to the governments that create them by attracting visitation which creates demand (local, regional, international), for goods and services: transportation, lodging, food service, guides, fuel, crafts, equipment, etc. Sometimes all it takes is a single question in a survey to collect basic economic data that can have great impact on planning and management.

Correspondingly, economic development sometimes conflicts with the visiting public's idea of a park. Such development may attract non-traditional or inappropriate activities. Some development may violate the public taste, symbolism, and imagery. Development can be perceived to be inconsistent or out of scale with the surroundings. Some developments threaten to destroy the entire web of economic interests that parks benefit. Economic and visitation impact studies can show both the negative and the beneficial side of these consequences, and the results can be used to protect the park and its image.

The world is cost conscious and so are governments. Because it costs money to protect the environment, conservationists have learned the language of economics. The conservation of resources can be explained and justified economically in many ways including the benefits of flood control, air quality benefits of habitat maintenance, the renewable revenues contributed by tourism, and the political stability associated with countries which have learned to behave as hosts to others.

Economic data is needed for the reasonable setting of fee schedules as well as the allocation of services (camping in versus outside the park). The development of parks and surrounding communities over decades may have been economically sustainable in the past, but is marginal in the present. Good economic data can help illuminate such conditions. Collecting credible economic data can also have many other advantages. In many areas, the economic impact of parks is greater than most of the industries surrounding them. By gathering economic information, governments as well as surrounding communities can be shown the value of investing and supporting the growth of park resources. This can allow parks to compete against other

industries for scarce governmental resources, on an economic basis as well as on an environmental basis. However, it must be stated that economic impact studies are usually best left to specialized professionals. It is often important to use professionals who are independent from the park.

The World Commission on Protected Areas has also developed guidelines for calculating the economic value of parks. These guidelines are available in both book and web format.

Economic impact studies are a logical companion to trip and visitor surveys (section 4.3.). We refer again to the Bent's Old Fort survey as an example of an economic study. Questions for economic assessments are covered in the Questionnaire Catalogue Chapter V.

REFERENCES

Bagri, A., J. Blockhus and F. Vorhies. 1999. Economic Values of Protected Areas. World Commission on Protected Areas, World Conservation Union, Gland, Switzerland.

4.5 STUDIES ON SATISFACTION: EVALUATING THE PARK, RESOURCES AND SERVICES

The measurement of visitor satisfaction with facilities and services is vital to the understanding of an agency's impact on visitors. Highly satisfied visitors give good recommendations to others. Highly satisfied visitors are more likely to return. Satisfied visitors are more likely to donate money to conservation and support political initiatives for conservation.

The measurement of satisfaction, however, is not a straightforward task of asking "are you satisfied?" Satisfaction is dependent upon many factors. One factor, for example, is a person's expectations. If a park visitor experienced a certain service or facility at one park, he often expects a similar service or facility at other parks. Another factor is the fulfilment of the need. All services and facilities are not needed by all visitors. Correspondingly, availability is another factor. Was the service or facility available on the day of the visit and at the time it was wanted? Other factors include appropriateness, performance quality rating, and importance. Each factor in satisfaction must be looked at and evaluated in the context of the others.

Parks are often weak in their systematic measurement of client satisfaction. As a result, the only options left for visitors to make their opinions known are to lodge a complaint, to disparage the park to others, to decide to never return, or all of the above. If the complaints are made a matter of record, the information can be useful for the manager. More often, dissatisfaction goes unrecorded as "ill-will" or "bad reputation."

A properly designed visitor satisfaction survey helps detect levels of satisfaction giving early warning of problem areas as well as giving seldom documented expressions of work that was appreciated. If these studies are repeated over time, the data can be tied back to associated indicators such as weather data, staffing and program levels, funding records, fee charges, or even road construction. All of this information gives management an operational understanding of how the park works. Operational understanding, in this case, means "when this happens (road construction, higher room rates, entrance delays, lack of signage), satisfaction rates go down." By knowing this in advance, it gives you time to make the proper adjustments to service levels in order to "make it up" to the customer. This can often lead to a customer becoming a repeat one. While it is best to "get it right the first time," it is also important to remember that if things do go wrong, it does present an opportunity to get that customer back. By "making up" for mistakes the customer knows you are looking out for their best interest. It is important to note that it has been found that a customer on average is worth many times the price of a single purchase.

It is well known in the service industry that satisfied people will pay a premium price for high quality. In the "park" industry one often sees dissatisfaction expressed in the costs of neglect, misuse, and vandalism. Promoting satisfaction can be seen as a way to combat the effects of visitor behaviour rooted in dissatisfaction.

Improved levels of service lead to several benefits for any organization, including parks. Better service leads to longer periods of stay in a park and to higher return rates. Parks receive much of their visitation due to word of mouth. It has been found that if people like a service, they will tell 3 others about the service. However, if they don't they will tell 11. Good service leads to recommendations from satisfied visitors. Satisfied visitors will leave accommodations in good order, and this will reduce cleaning and preparation time. Positive feedback helps staff morale. Better morale leads to increased productivity and lower costs.

To measure satisfaction, start by asking the visitor to rate their experience with a service or facility. One approach is to list the service in the questionnaire and then ask visitors to rate the park performance with the service on a scale (e.g., excellent, above average, average, below average, very poor). Each level can be numbered, from 1 for excellent to 5 for very poor. After the data is collected, the numbers can be averaged so that management can get a numerical score for the performance rating of each service.

Visitor ratings of performance, however, may be misleading to the extent that visitors hold various levels of importance for different services. To measure satisfaction, you also have to determine the importance associated with the services rated by each visitor. For example, the visitors may say that a park is doing a very good job at something that is not very important to them or maybe not even needed or used. To measure importance, you list the service and ask visitors how important the item is. A scale could be used with options ranging from extremely important, important, neutral, not important, to not at all important. Each level can be numbered, 1 for very important, to 5 for not at

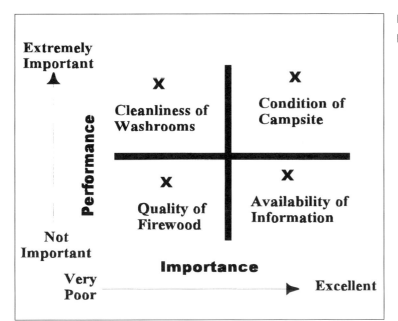

FIGURE 3: IMPORTANCE VS. PERFORMANCES MATRIX

TABLE 7: CAMPERS' PRIORITIES VS. PARK PERFORMANCE

Park Services and Facilities	Importance	Performance	Gap
Cleanliness of Washrooms	1.47	2.21	-.74
Condition of Campsite	1.61	1.95	-.34
Quality of Firewood	2.25	2.46	-.21
Availability of Information	2.07	2.04	+.03

all important. After the data is collected, the numbers can be averaged so that the manager can get a numerical score for the importance of each service.

Because people often rate services they do not use, a question on whether a service or facility was used or not used is posed to remove this population from the scores. What is left are two scales, one for performance and one for importance.

To compare the visitor's ideas on the importance of a service with the park's performance on that service, the two figures are compared. For example, if a park got a mark of 2.5 for importance of a facility, say the cleanliness of washrooms, but a lower score of 4.5 on the performance of the facility, then a large importance – performance gap is clearly present.

Subsequently, the manager must look at the reasons for this facility not performing to the level of importance given by the visitor.

Table 7 shows importance rankings compared to performance rankings from a large sample of campers from Ontario Provincial Parks in Canada. Figure 3 shows the same data as found in Table 7, but in graph format. One can clearly see from a financial perspective, that most funds should be allocated to the cleanliness of the washrooms, as this service is high in importance and lower in performance. Quality of firewood, while low in performance is also low in importance. Therefore, significant funds should not be allocated to this area. However, a performance measure on its own, without the importance measure, could lead management to invest as many new funds toward firewood, as toward the washrooms. Condition of the campsite is high in both importance and

TABLE 8: IMPORTANCE/PERFORMANCE OF LODGES IN SERENGETTI NATIONAL PARK

Type of Accommodation	Mean Importance of Accommodation	Mean Performance of Accommodation	Service Quality Gap
Sopa Lodge	1.7	1.48	0.22
Serena Lodge	1.84	1.33	0.51
Seronera Lodge	2.33*	2.42*	-0.09

*Difference is statistically significant

performance (although a small gap does exist), indicating relatively successful service quality management in this area.

Availability of information is ranked as low in importance but high in performance. If an operating budget is to be reallocated toward washroom upkeep, this would be a good area to decrease spending. Clearly, the addition of a measure of importance provides essential information for not only elevating levels of service quality, but also in maximizing the allocation of funds.

An example of the use of importance and performance measures in a study of lodge accommodation in Serengetti National Park is shown in Table 8. Statistical tests, using analysis of variance, found that guests who stay at the Seronera Wildlife Lodge place a significantly lower importance on the type of accommodation than do the guests of the Sopa and Serena Lodges. In addition, the Seronera Wildlife Lodge guests assign a lower performance ranking to their accommodation. When service quality gaps are analyzed, all guests are satisfied with this private sector accommodation within the park. If performance alone was viewed, a manager would incorrectly assume that guests are unsatisfied with the Seronera Wildlife Lodge. The data show that lodge visitors to this national park sought differing service levels at each of the lodges. This case study shows the necessity of measuring both importance and performance, and calculating the difference between the two to check for service quality gaps.

There are many ways to measure aspects of satisfaction from the user point of view: usefulness, expectations, need fulfilment, quality rating (positive-negative scale), appropriateness, and importance. In addition, there are many circumstances which may be added together (justifiably or not) by users when evaluating factors such as weather, crowdedness, delays, etc. The best way to deal with such possible complexity is to be as specific as possible about what is being rated.

In addition to the many factors associated with satisfaction, there are many outside factors which may be added together (justifiably or not) in the minds of users when they evaluate services and facilities such as weather, crowdedness, delays, etc. The best way to deal with such possible complexity is to be as specific as possible about what is being rated and to undertake ratings across a broad spectrum of parks.

It is important that after conducting a satisfaction survey, the park visitors are told the outcome. Actions that prove to the visitors that their comments and concerns are being dealt with are needed. In this manner, people being surveyed can see the results of previous surveys, and will be more likely to complete any upcoming surveys. Appendix 4 shows an example, from Parks Canada, of feedback from a camper satisfaction survey. This document was posted on the campground's bulletin board for all campers to read.

These GUIDELINES cannot provide all the background and intricacies of park visitor satisfaction measurement. However, it is important for park managers to recognize this important component of an ADVANCED park public use measurement program.

REFERENCES

LeBoeuf, M. 1987. How to Win Customers and Keep Them for Life. California: Berkley Press.

4.6 STUDIES OF CROWDING AND CONFLICT

The quality of a park experience partly depends on the fit between the resource and the people who use it. Consequently the analysis of a park experience may include a focus on crowding, interpersonal conflict, and, generally on the ability of the park to support people and their needs. Attempts to set use limits based on notions of crowdedness have generated substantial controversy and even law suits. Rudimentary information is needed to determine the nature of public sensitivity to crowds and the publics involved.

Appendix 5 contains a questionnaire covering a variety of issues, as all field studies invariably do. The Grand Teton National Park Snake River Survey was directed at users of a specific area of the park with respect to crowds, park policy, development direction, and the visit experience. Compared to the Bent's Old Fort questionnaire, the Snake River Survey is complicated. However, this study was conducted by trained interviewers who were familiar with the form and prepared to clarify visitor understanding of the questions. It would be a challenge to convert this survey to a form that could be self-administered by the public and keep it on one page.

Notice the "core questions" about the interview conditions at the top of the form. Also, at the end of the form there is a space given for "anything else about your visit you would like park management to know about?" This last item is a good way to close the interview and offers an

opportunity to collect a variety of comments and ideas. The content of this type of study is covered in the Questionnaire Catalogue Chapter VI.

4.7 STUDIES OF ENVIRONMENTAL ATTITUDES, BELIEFS, EXPECTATIONS, PERCEPTIONS

As the demand for outdoor recreation and visitation to parks and protected areas increases, a growing number of managers will need to develop policies which guide or restrict visitor use to protect the park resources.

Changing visitation demand will also impact park communities both negatively and positively. The attitudes that develop in the community are important to park managers. Knowledge of changing community beliefs is critical to keeping the park a member in good standing with local people. Any park which remains isolated from the surrounding political economy will not be able to protect itself from unfavorable development, legislation, funding, etc. The place to start is with a methodical understanding of public attitudes. Such understanding may not come from the media or elected officials who sometimes reflect the most colorful or loudest opinions. Such influences may not be in the overall best interests of the community in general, especially if misinformation, rumor, or gossip surround park related issues.

More attention will also be given to the existing belief systems of visitors and the new information which can be conveyed to the visitor by the park. Research has shown that environmental attitudes and knowledge about one's own negative impact on the environment are critical in mitigating backlash to such policies. Many of the questions in this section have been taken from the "new environmental paradigm" (NEP) scale developed by Dunlap and Van Liere (1978). Questions about environmental attitudes are found in the Questionnaire Catalogue Chapter IX.

REFERENCES

Dunlap, R. and K. Van Liere. 1978. The New Environmental Paradigm. Journal of Environmental Education 9 (4): 10-19.

Noe, F. and R. Snow. 1989. Hispanic Cultural Influence on Environmental Concern. Journal of Environmental Education 21 (2):27-34.

4.8 STUDIES OF PUBLIC VALUES, WANTS AND NEEDS

At a public meeting about the development of the Cuyahoga National Recreation Area of the United States of America, the public demanded the National Park Service "clean up the Cuyahoga River". Cleaning up the river was not within the agency's power but a central clearinghouse for information about river cleanup and contact agencies was set up and maintained by the park. The park understood the public message and took what action it could. Everyone was satisfied. What a disaster it would have been if the agency had dismissed the request or declared it outside of its authority. To understand public values, wants, and needs you have to look beyond the words and understand the intent.

Managers need and use a wide variety of information in making policy, planning, and managerial decisions. Studies of public issues, policies, and alternatives enable management to avoid unintended consequences of direct action. These studies provide additional information about public intent, the depth of public understanding or misunderstanding of technicalities, and provide an opportunity to collect background information that can enlighten management. The content of this type of study are covered in the Questionnaire Catalogue Chapter VII.

4.9 STUDIES OF RESOURCE UTILIZATION – CREEL SURVEYS – SPECIFIC POPULATION STUDIES

Certain kinds of information are only available from visitors such as the number of fish taken from park lakes and streams, number of people encountered in backcountry areas, conditions of

resources they may have experienced or services they have utilized while in the park. These studies are usually specific to areas, activities, or types of visitors. If the data are logically required to deal with the issue, the associated study should be based on data from all park visitors, that is any visitor during an annual management cycle. If the study is exploratory (seeks to discover if a more formal study should be attempted), the effort should be limited to a single, continuous data collection contacting as many visitors as is practical within a few hours or days. The content of this type of study is covered in the Questionnaire Catalogue Chapter X, Creel Surveys.

4.10 STUDIES OF VISITOR TYPES (MARKETS, RECREATION LIFESTYLE, AND COMMUNITY STUDIES)

Studies on visitor types or submarkets are usually part of economic and commercial studies or associated with strategic planning and forecasting. The content of this type of study are covered in the Questionnaire Catalog Chapter VIII.

4.11 COMMUNICATING THE RESULTS

It is important that the results of visitor studies be communicated to the users of information, at several levels. The full studies will be compiled and made available to those most in need of sophisticated analyses, such as tourism analysts. However, it is important to not forget the large number of planners, managers and field staff who can best utilize a short summary. Appendix 4 provides an example of feedback to the park campers, the people who filled out the survey. Appendix 6 provides an example of a summary document for park staff. This example summarizes the results of a study of the users of a day-use area in Georgian Bay Islands National Park in Canada. Virtually any staff member involved in the management of this day-use area could benefit from reading this short, but carefully crafted document.

CHAPTER 5

DATA

5.0 INTRODUCTION

Visitor studies depend upon the collection of data about park visitors. Most of this is collected by surveys, where visitors are asked questions. The answers provide the data needed to answer the management questions. It is usually not possible to collect sufficient information from all visitors, so a sample of the visitors is used to represent the large group.

5.1 HOW TO COLLECT A GOOD SAMPLE

While much can be said about sampling and the statistical considerations that are involved, when it comes to collecting a sample, the weather, the availability of staff, and the absence of other crises dictate what can be done. Given a variety of impediments faced by park managers, a simple random sample consisting of numerous but limited efforts to collect data will likely result in the best sample. A big sample is not necessarily a good sample. For our purposes, the best sample is one which results from short collection efforts spread throughout the month, often at several locations around the park.

The following steps are for collecting a sample of visitors at a location within a park for a given month. The sample described is a sample of time periods and representative of visitors for the month when it is collected.

1. Make a calendar for the month the study is to be conducted.

2. Divide each day into 3 periods of equal time intervals during daylight when visitors are present, e.g. from 7:00 A.M. to 11:00 A.M.,

11:00 A.M. to 3:00 P.M., and 3:00 P.M. to 7:00 P.M.

3. Take a telephone book and open to any page, pick any column of numbers and mark a number on any line. Look at the last number on the line. If that number matches any last digit of a date on your calendar in the column of Sundays, it is a sample day. Move to the next row in the telephone book and see if it matches any other last digit of a date in the Sunday column. Continue until you have marked 3 Sundays in the sample month. Do the same for every other day of the week on your calendar. When you are finished, you have picked a simple, random sample of 21 hours that represent all the visitors for the month.

4. Start collecting data for approximately one hour anytime during the first A.M. period on the first randomly sampled day and rotate to the middle time period on the second sample day and last time period on the third sample day. Start over with the first sample period on the fourth day, etc. The sampling effort will involve 21 hours of work.

The method described is for a self-weighted sample, based on approximately one hour of data collection per sample period. The sampling method assumes collection of answers to a small number of questions by face-to-face interview. If the collection takes more than two to three minutes or if the location is saturated with visitors, more than one hour may be required. The objective is to complete about 20 survey instruments during the period when the greatest number of visitors is present at the chosen site. If it takes an hour and a half to complete 20 survey instruments due to the number of questions, all sample periods should last for that length of time to get a self-weighted sample. That means more survey instruments will be collected when visitor volume is high than when it is low. If attendance is so high that data collectors are overwhelmed by visitors, it is no longer self-weighting and more help needs to be assigned to the task.

The method described produces a sample representing all visitors at a location within a park for a month. If the location is a campground, the data collected might be considered a study of campground users. If the park also has a visitor center and a lot of day-use visitors who do not camp, a sample from the visitor center is also needed. If one needs a sample which is representative of all visitors to the park within a month, repeat the basic procedure for all major gathering points with different people, using the same sampling plan at each of those points or generate a different sampling plan for each point. To collect a sample of all park visitors for a year, conduct a sampling for a month during each major season.

There are other ways of going about doing a study. For example, as a general convention, most studies dealing with survey information aim for a statistical error not greater than 5% at a 95% confidence level, based on a question with two answers [yes-no] where the findings yield 50% "yes" and 50% "no" [Backstrom and Hursh-Cesar, 1981:75]. Such conditions indicate a sample of 384 answers which usually means completed interviews or questionnaires. That is a way to start solving the problem of matching management requirements to a study design, and where most people stop. The answers to survey questions, however, usually include more than yes-no answers and are often skewed on several but not all possible answers. To the extent that this happens and to the extent that the needs of management become critical for one or more possible answers, the sample designed for such basic and simple requirements becomes inadequate. For example, if a sample of 384 is

selected and management becomes interested in the differences between answers from one part of the park to another, the data are statistically inadequate.

For a complete treatment of survey design and implementation, many people recommend Don Dillman's (1978) book.

REFERENCES

Backstrom, C.H., Hursh-Cesar, G. 1981. Survey Research. Macmillan Publishing Co., New York, U.S.A.

Dillman, Don. 1978. Mail and Telephone Surveys: The Total Design Method. John Wiley and Sons, New York, U.S.A.

Yuan, S., Maiorano, B., Yuan, M. 1995. Techniques and Equipment for Gathering Visitor Use Data on Recreation Sites. August, U.S. Forest Service Publication No. 9523-2838-MTDC, Missoula, Montana, U.S.A.

5.2 METHODS OF COLLECTING DATA

5.2.1 PERSONAL INTERVIEWS

The personal interview is the preferred method of collecting information from visitors when they can be contacted at gathering places in the park. The willingness of travellers to give information to park staff is quite high relative to other methods (80% or better). Usually, such high rates of completion make efforts to study non-response bias unnecessary. Most parks have staff who are available and trained to communicate with the public so this activity is natural for them. This method is cost effective on the basis of simplicity, completion and accuracy.

5.2.2 REGISTRATION CARDS

Chapter 3 discussed visitor registration as an opportunity to collect information. Registration cards are intended to be completed by visitors and returned immediately to the park staff. The card may record the date, time and in-park destination for public safety purposes, serve as a record of visits, establish adjustment factors (e.g., persons per vehicle), indicate payment of fees, and communicate to visitors basic hazards and how to deal with them. By designing different versions of the same basic registration form, a number of park operational needs can be served without great delay to the public. Because such forms are intended to be completed on the spot, they can be checked over for completeness.

5.2.3 MAILBACK QUESTIONNAIRES

It may not be practical to interview people or attempt to get all visitors to register. A questionnaire can be mailed to visitors for completion after their visit to the park. Generally, it is possible to collect more data from a mailback questionnaire than is polite to ask in an interview or convenient to collect from a registration form. Visitors are asked if they would be willing to complete the questionnaire and, if so, give their home address and date when they expect to be home. The questionnaire is sent later.

By the time many visitors return home, they may change their minds about completing the questionnaire. The expected return rate of the original questionnaires is 40 to 50%. Issuing reminders and second copies can improve the return rate by about 10% for each effort up to about 60%. Higher return rates are unusual. That leaves lingering questions about people who do not reply at all. For those who do fill it out, the time difference between the park experience and the experience of reading questions is expected to result in errors of recall. On the basis of cost versus accuracy, this method is relatively expensive.

5.2.4 TELEPHONE INTERVIEWS

A telephone interview can be arranged with the visitor at the park just as with the mailback questionnaire. Telephone calls are often made randomly to residents of a community as part of community studies or studies of visitors and non-visitors. Calls are often placed as a form of follow-up to a questionnaire non-respondent.

Long distance telephone interviews may not be practical or cost effective. Calls must be placed during appropriate time differentials. Unless

arranged in advance in person or by mail, calls to the home can be viewed as an invasion of privacy and create hostility.

5.2.5 MIXED METHODOLOGIES

Counting visits is a necessary part of the basic job of park operation, resource and visitor protection. Knowing something about visitors helps keep visit counts accurate and serves a variety of other purposes. Learning about visitors is work. The most cost effective program will probably be some mixture of counting by instruments, campground counts by observation, registration in conjunction with fee payments, and the occasional representative sample to help understand how the other areas relate to each other. By using mixed methods, you create a situation where you have something called "triangulation". Triangulation simply refers to using more that one type of data collection to make sure what you are seeing in the data is accurate. It is like having three people telling you something, rather than just one. It is a way to lend credibility to your findings. Therefore, a better system will use a mixture of methodologies.

5.3 WHO WILL DO THE STUDY?

If a survey must be done, the lowest cost is to have the park staff do the work. The higher cost is to import labor hired by an outside contractor. The method recommended here is the brief face-to-face interview between the park staff and a visitor. The maximum time of delay for a visitor will vary from culture to culture and by content of the instrument. In many western countries people like to recount their experience and sometimes do too much talking, taking the valuable time of the park staff! Five to six minutes of interview should be enough to get sufficient information from a well-designed list of questions. Always remember that the park can do another survey another time. If park staff are accustomed to communicating with park visitors, the only thing they have to become familiar with are the questions, codes and any special interpretations in use.

Some park agencies hire students to conduct visitor surveys. The students are carefully trained to conduct the surveys. With standardized survey instruments, well-designed data collection procedures and substantial levels of training, part-time employees can be used for these tasks.

For specialized work, such as economic impact studies or service satisfaction monitoring, it may be best to utilize professionals from outside the park agency. It is not possible for any agency to maintain staffing with all the required expertise for all types of visitor surveys. In addition, for undertaking studies that are politically charged, outside contractors have a level of independence that may be necessary.

5.4 SURVEY DESIGN, PRE-CODING AND PRETEST

For survey instruments to be used in the field, designers should be sensitive to the user. Little things like wind and sunlight can ruin or distort the most carefully designed study. Wind will blow paper around. Some of it will get lost. Wind will delay the time it takes to complete what should be a simple task. Sunlight can reflect off shiny paper and cause items to be skipped or make items hard to read. The texture of some paper makes it hard to mark or easy to smear which could cause errors in coding or editing data. It is important to tell staff involved with studies that completed survey instruments are valuable pieces of paper. They represent an investment of time on the part of the government and citizens to get something done. That time is irreplaceable.

Questionnaires of only a single page are easiest to use and process. Single page surveys can be easily reproduced. Multiple page surveys can come apart, making it difficult to match up information that belongs together. If a questionnaire takes up more than a page, it is probably too long. Reducing the size of print helps put more on paper, but it makes it more difficult to read by people with poor vision. If a lot of information needs to be put on a page, it is better to use the margins. Over-size paper can be folded in half to make a seamless two-page survey which is still manageable.

Instruments can be subdivided into different versions to ease the pain of administration and burden on the respondent. The different versions are mixed together. Each version has a common core of questions followed by sections that vary from one to another.

The amount of time it takes to give answers needs to be kept to a minimum. For face-to-face interviews, it is desirable to limit the time as much as possible. The best is less than 7 minutes, but this may vary from country to country. Designers are usually less concerned about completion time with self-administered questionnaires and the high non-response rates show it.

Answers to some questions will always be hard to express. This is less of a problem with questionnaires than with interviews. In the case of interviews, a good practice is to make a handout showing a map or giving a list of answers. You have to be careful in doing this however, not to lead respondents to answer what they think you want to hear rather than what they are really thinking.

The use of cartoon-like illustrations is often more effective than representational maps. Artistic enhancement can communicate the image of importance, ease of completion, fun, legal significance or other attributes one might want to attribute to the form.

5.5 QUALITY CONTROL DURING STUDY, EDITING

It is important that the data collected be accurately tabulated and reported. Checks should be built into the system so that data is rechecked several times to maintain accuracy. Inaccurate data is worse than no data because it leads to erroneous conclusions that appear to be correct.

5.6 DESIGNING YOUR OWN QUESTIONS

Designing survey questions is difficult. However, many people not trained in the social sciences do not recognize the importance of very careful design and testing of survey questions. If questions not found in the standardized catalogue are required, the following process should be used.

The objective of the question must be clear. What important information is required? The question should be worded in clear, logical language. It should be pretested, first with other park staff, and later on a small sample of the intended audience. After these pretests, the wording should be carefully evaluated and changes made if required. Only after all these pretests, should a new question be used.

It is important to use survey wording that can be easily translated into other languages. Many parks attract international visitors, and it is important to utilize survey instruments in the language most suitable for the visitor.

5.7 POST-CODING, RECODING, DATA PROCESSING, REPORTS AND PRESENTATION

Typically the data is collected on paper surveys. This is then input by a person into a spreadsheet program for tabulation. When complex statistical analyses are required, specialized statistical programs should be used. Much of the newer word processing software enables tables and graphs to be dynamically linked to the spreadsheet data base. This means that as new data is added to the data base, or new calculations are done, the tables in the report are automatically updated.

New technologies for collecting data are proving to be very useful. One of these includes optical reading of the paper survey by machine so as to reduce the need for personal data input through a keyboard. Another and exciting method is direct input into the computer by the survey respondent. In this approach the park visitor sits in front of a computer that displays the survey questions. The responses to the questions are entered into the survey through the keyboard or through clicks of the mouse. These responses are immediately saved into a database. With the onset of the world wide web, it is possible to have respondents fill out the survey directly into their computer at home or work. They then send the completed questionnaire to the main data base by their web connection.

With the properly designed spreadsheet or statistical program, it is possible to get survey results quickly. These results can be distributed in report format, or as electronic reports. With the power of the world wide web attached to powerful personal computers, it is possible to have reports submitted to key people in a park or in a parks' agency in just a few hours or days after the data was collected.

5.8 LONG TERM STORAGE OF THE DATA

The collected data is valuable. The opportunity to collect this data is gone forever. Therefore, the permanent storage of the data must be assured. After a time, the paper copies of surveys can be recycled. The copies of final reports should be stored permanently in a library, both in the central office and in the park. The computer files are the easiest to lose. Multiple copies of the original data bases should be made, and stored in different locales. Never leave the data files on just one computer. It is easy for this machine to be stolen, be recycled or be lost. Coding books and the descriptions of the content of the data bases should be stored with the computer files.

DATA PROCESSING COMPUTER PROGRAMS

6.0 INTRODUCTION

Chapter 6 covers the uses of computers to ease the tasks of public use reporting. Material covered here will need to be enlarged and updated at frequent intervals. The availability of programs will eventually be through telecommunications and the internet. For the present, programs are available from suppliers as indicated.

Many useful programs can be managed by people with limited experience with computers if they have been set up and prepared for use by the novice. Generic programs such as spreadsheets (e.g., Excel, Quattro Pro, or Lotus 1-2-3) can be operated at a basic level by attentive people with little experience but most applications require advanced skills and experience. Central offices and centers of higher learning can provide priceless assistance to parks by tailoring generic programs to do various jobs for park managers including public use reporting. Two of the following programs (ParkStat and EZForms Database) are such bi-level programs . . . bi-level in that they are somewhat involved to set up but easy to use on an every day basis by field staff.

6.1 RECUSE 1.0

RECREATION USE (RECUSE 1.0) is the name of a computer program developed by the United States Forest Service (Department of Agriculture) to enable its staff to produce random samples of days for visitor surveys. The user provides the start and finish dates, names of sites involved and the sampling confidence level needed. The computer calculates and displays a simple or stratified random selection of days. The program also accepts field data collected from sampling and calculates basic statistics such as confidence limits, coefficient of variation, standard error, estimation of variance, etc. The program runs on older DOS types of computer. Documentation and programs are available from the United States Forest Service in Missoula, Montana, U.S.A.

6.2 QDATA

QData is a package of data analysis programs prepared for the National Park Service by Dean Savage of the Sociology Department, Queens College, New York and Jesse Reichler, Department of Computer Science, University of Illinois, United States of America. It is a bi-level program (also called tier-programming) intended to be set up by someone with established computer skills and some experience, but used by others with little or no prior computer experience.

QData is a program that displays the variables measured by park visitor surveys and allows the user to "tag" those which are of interest at the moment. The selections can then be viewed as tables or graphic displays. The program was designed to enable park staff to answer most of their basic statistical questions without consulting statisticians. The program also enables a park staff to save screens of data for display as a "slide show." The program was designed to replace paper reports in recognition of the emergent needs of park staff for data. The program is designed to help the staff connect immediate management and planning problems with visitor use statistics.

The Department of Sociology at Queens College of the City University of New York have prepared a website that includes DOS freeware program elements of ParkStat (QData, a data management program and QStats, a data exploration and analysis program) as well as related sociological information. It is all available free for downloading from the web site at http://www.soc.qc.edu/QC_Software/qdata.html.

6.3 FORMS AND DATABASE MANAGERS

There is a category of software called forms manager. This program enables a user to design a form on the computer screen. Data is input to the data base through the form. There are several good commercial programs available. One commonly used by parks is called EZ-Forms. EZ forms database program is a forms' manager and database management system. It is a bi-level program (also called tier-programming) intended to be set up by someone. It is available as a shareware program. Information is available on the world wide web at http://ez-forms.com.

However, many database management programs have form management software built in. For example, Microsoft Excel 97, the spreadsheet program, and Microsoft Access 97, the database management program, each have the capability for the design of input forms. These forms are portrayed on the computer screen and look just like survey forms. When a person inputs data into these forms, it is placed automatically directly into the relevant database. Recently, world wide web form managers are becoming widely available. These enable a person with web access to input data directly into a data base both locally and remotely. This capability is extremely useful for widely distributed park units within a park system. Each park can input their visitor use data directly into a remote data base at a central office, using the world wide web, thereby providing rapid access and distribution of the important data.

6.4 COMMERCIAL STATISTICS PACKAGES

For advanced data management and analysis there are many sophisticated software packages available. SPSS is available for both mainframe and personal computers. Its use requires good levels of knowledge of both statistics and computers. The personal computer version is useful for small offices without access to a mainframe computer and the associated data processing department. The world wide web address for the company that develops and sells SPSS is http://www.spss.com. The software is available worldwide through computer retailers.

SAS is another useful program, with similar capabilities to SPSS. The world wide web address for the company that develops and sells SAS is http://www.sas.com. The software is available through commercial software outlets.

Systat is a commercial statistical package that is less expensive that SPSS or SAS. Some park tourism analysts find that it has sufficient capability for their needs. Systat is sold by the SPSS company. Information on the software can be found on the SPSS Web Page at http://www.spss.com/software/science/SYSTAT.

CHAPTER 7

MEASUREMENT OF PUBLIC USE OF MARINE PROTECTED AREAS — Kenneth J. Vrana

7.0 INTRODUCTION

The designation of marine protected areas has become a common strategy employed worldwide to improve conservation of natural resources and preservation of cultural heritage, and to enhance opportunities for coastal recreation and tourism. The term MARINE PROTECTED AREA is commonly used to describe all areas established by governments for protection and management of ocean, freshwater, coastal, and underwater resources.

Many of the issues associated with measurement of public use at land-based parks also exist at MARINE PROTECTED AREAS (MPAs). In most cases,

there is a lack of comprehensive information on public uses that can be applied with confidence for management and development of these areas. This includes the types of visitors, their activities, knowledge of the resource, satisfaction with recreation experiences, and expenditures during their trip. Information on different user groups is often important in resource management because changes in one group, such as increases in the number of personal watercraft operators, can have significant impacts on other recreational groups and the marine environment. While some information is available on selected activities tied to key industries such as boating and fishing, there is little data on water-based recreation activities such as swimming, snorkeling, scuba

Bruce Peninsula National Park, Canada

Marine protected areas often have multiple land and water entry points, making visitation recording a challenging task.

diving, and beach use. Comparison of public use among marine protected areas is often hindered by inconsistent definitions and criteria, and gaps in information.

There are many opportunities to improve the measurement of public use of marine protected areas. These opportunities are related to increases in the use of coastal areas for recreation and tourism, concerns about cumulative impact on marine resources, and awareness that monitoring of public use is an important function of resource management. A variety of scientific methods is available for measuring public use of MPAs. Most of these methods apply to marine protected areas as well as land-based parks. The challenges are to effectively adapt these methods to often difficult coastal environments, and to design efficient methods for measurement of water-based recreation and tourism.

The primary purpose of this chapter is to increase awareness of marine protected areas and the need for measurement of public use. Information presented should be viewed as a preliminary description of marine protected areas, visitor activities within these areas, and distinguishing characteristics of use and management. The chapter concludes with general guidelines and potential methods for measuring public use of MPAs.

7.1 MARINE PROTECTED AREAS

Fort Jefferson National Monument, United States of America and Green Island National Park, Australia are commonly cited as the first marine protected areas. Both were established in the 1930s. Over 1,000 marine protected areas have now been designated by governments worldwide. Most MPAs have been established for multiple purposes of environmental protection, historic preservation, enhancement of recreation, and tourism-based economic development. Some have become worldwide tourism destinations (e.g.,

Florida Keys National Marine Sanctuary in the U.S.A. and Great Barrier Reef Marine Park in Australia) that enhance the economic well-being of nearby coastal communities. Many generate revenues from user fees and sales to visitors that are used in support of park operations.

The name used to identify marine protected areas varies widely by nation and within nations. The names usually include a reference to the physical environment (e.g., marine, estuary, aquatic, coastal, underwater) and a reference to the type of administrative unit (e.g., park, sanctuary, reserve, preserve). A distinction is often made between the purpose of marine PARKS and the purpose of marine RESERVES. Parks are commonly viewed as more focused on the needs of people; reserves are commonly viewed as focused on resource preservation and the recruitment of aquatic life (i.e., conceptual equivalent to land-based "wilderness"). In practice, it is often difficult to differentiate between the operations of a park and a reserve. The key document in determining the actual purposes of each area is its MANAGEMENT PLAN.

The World Conservation Union (IUCN) has developed different categories of protected areas based on their purposes for management. A number of organizations have developed guidelines specifically for the management and development of marine protected areas.

Large concentrations and important examples of natural and cultural resources often are managed within a marine protected area. Natural resources may include coral reefs, other aquatic life, and geological features. Cultural materials may include shipwrecks, other historic sites, and prehistoric artifacts. MPAs often include shorelands and land-based facilities, services, and visitor programs. They may also contain human-built underwater structures, and intentionally sunken natural and cultural materials (e.g., artificial reefs to improve aquatic habitat, shipwrecks to enhance recreational experiences).

The many "waterparks" owned and operated by private businesses are not considered in this paper. These areas are generally recreation intensive and have an emphasis on development of facilities and entertainment programs.

7.2 TYPES OF VISITOR ACTIVITIES

The use of coastal areas throughout the world for recreation and tourism has increased substantially in recent years. Diversification of coastal recreation activities has contributed to this increase and significantly influenced tourism development and resource management. The diversification of these activities has been associated with changes in consumer preferences as well as development of marine technology.

Participants in water-based recreation commonly perceive marine protected areas as tourism destinations. Management organizations and businesses near these areas often promote compatible recreation and tourism activities within MPAs. Water-based recreation is usually segmented in social research by the type of activity. The type of activity is often differentiated by mode of access and specialization of the participant. Types of water-based recreation activities used in survey research include the following:

WATER-BASED RECREATION ACTIVITIES

Boating (motorized)	Water-skiing
Boating (non-motorized)	Sailboarding
Fishing	Para-sailing
Swimming	Viewing wildlife
Scuba diving	Nature study
Snorkeling	Visiting historical sites

The mode of access to natural and cultural resources within MPAs may include private automobile, public transportation (e.g., trains, buses), motorcycle, bicycle, horse or other domestic animal, and foot travel (hiking) to SHORELANDS, and by boat on the SURFACE WATERS of the area. Mode of access for boats can be

further differentiated by private, rental, charter, tour or cruise boat. Scuba diving and snorkeling equipment, and recreational submersibles provide access to features underwater.

Specialization within boating may include the powerboat, sailboat, personal watercraft (i.e., jet-ski), canoe, kayak, and other small craft. Specialization within fishing may include hand-line, casting with an artificial lure, bait-casting, fly-fishing, trolling, surf-fishing, and off-shore or deep-sea fishing. Some researchers consider specialization of swimming to include snorkeling and scuba diving. Recreational scuba divers often perceive specialization by difficulty of dive plan and the use of technologies (e.g., mixed gas, rebreathers) to make a distinction between "technical" scuba diving and recreational diving.

Sport or recreational scuba diving is a relatively new, water-based activity for which managers of MPAs are in need of information. Divers are often vocal advocates of marine protected areas and have become influential stakeholders in the management and development of these areas. For these reasons, a brief profile of recreational scuba diving and divers is presented in the following section. Some commercial and subsistence uses of MPAs will be identified after the profile of recreational scuba diving.

RECREATIONAL SCUBA DIVING
The development of sport or recreational scuba diving is part of the trend in diversification of coastal recreation and tourism. Recreational diving began soon after the invention of SCUBA (self-contained underwater breathing apparatus) in France during the late 1940s. Today, an estimated six to seven million people worldwide are ACTIVE participants in recreational scuba diving for a variety of purposes. An active participant is defined in this case as a certified scuba diver who participates in one or more recreational diving-related activities during the past twelve months.

Estimates of recreational scuba diving activity worldwide vary among certification organizations, the diving industry in general, and the social research community. The variation is due, in large part, to (1) inconsistent definitions of participation, (2) a high attrition rate among newly certified divers that is not well understood, (3) an inadequate amount and quality of scientific survey and marketing research, and (4) lack of coordination among members of the recreational diving industry to produce reliable profiles of diver market segments and estimates of diving activities. In addition, there is a lack of scientific information for most tourism destinations on recreational scuba divers and diving activities that can be used with confidence in management and development of marine protected areas.

Profiles of active recreational scuba divers indicate that they possess relatively high household incomes, educational attainment, and propensity for travel. Expenditures by recreational scuba divers have in many cases, contributed significantly to the economies of coastal communities near dive destinations. Surveys of scuba divers indicate that coral reefs and shipwrecks are the most popular attractions for recreational diving within marine protected areas, and within a nation's territorial seas in general. Abundant aquatic life is probably the primary draw to coral reefs, and provides additional aesthetic benefits to divers visiting shipwrecks.

Access to underwater environments by recreational scuba divers, however, may result in (1) negative impacts to natural and cultural resources, (2) conflicts among users, and (3) often complex decisions involving resource management and tourism development. Negative impacts to natural and cultural resources may include loss of coral or cultural materials due to theft, and localized damage to coral reefs, certain micro habitats, and historic shipwrecks due to vandalism and the unintentional actions of visitors. These impacts over time (i.e., cumulative impacts) may diminish the attractiveness of a site for recreation and tourism. Conflicts among

users may arise from congestion on a popular dive site or incompatible uses such as hook-and-line fishing and scuba diving on the same reef or historic shipwreck.

Actions taken by resource managers in response to these negative impacts and the conflicts among users may include increased efforts in visitor communications, educational programs within local communities, and more active law enforcement. Many of these actions, such as more active law enforcement, have implications for the marketing of recreational diving at a MPA and for private investment in tourism development at nearby communities. In nearly all cases, information about public use is needed to enhance the effectiveness and efficiency of actions taken by stakeholders in resource management and tourism development.

COMMERCIAL AND SUBSISTENCE USES
Other public uses of marine protected areas may be allowed under permit by management authorities for commercial purposes or subsistence of local residents. Subsistence activities commonly involve fishing, but may include other traditional uses of marine resources within the MPA. Permits may be issued for the following types of activities within marine protected areas, under certain conditions:

Tour boat operations (recreation and tourism)
Charter and rental boat operations (recreation and tourism)
Guide services (recreation and tourism)
Commercial fishing (fin-fish and shellfish)
Collection of marine resources (tropical fish, coral, pearls, shells)
Salvage of historic shipwrecks
Mining
Oil and gas extraction

The permit requirements may include reporting of park entrants, description of work or subsistence activities, and other more specialized information. The quality of public use information derived from these permits is dependent upon the ability of resource managers to (1) identify ALL commercial and subsistence users, and (2) facilitate compliance by these users in providing the required information.

7.3 DISTINGUISHING CHARACTERISTICS OF USE

There are certain characteristics of use that distinguish marine protected areas from land-based parks. These characteristics include the following:

Focus on water-based recreation activities
Prevalent use of boats as a mode of access
Open access to public resources
Dependence on marine technologies

Although many marine protected areas may include beaches and other shorelands within their administrative boundaries, the focus of public use is primarily water-based recreation activities, especially boating, fishing, swimming, snorkeling, and scuba diving. Boats of various types are the principal mode of access to marine resources of interest to participants in water-based recreation. Access to marine resources within MPAs can be characterized as "open" because of the numerous travel routes available to visitors aboard boats. In addition, the seaward or water boundaries of marine protected areas usually are not marked in any fashion by management authorities. Boaters require navigation charts and marine technologies such as a global positioning system (GPS) or fathometer (depth sounder) to determine their position within or outside of the marine protected area.

These characteristics of use of marine protected areas present special challenges to management organizations prepared primarily for land-based park operations. In particular, the collection of public use information at recreation and tourism attractions within a MPA is severely restricted if management authorities do not possess the boats, marine technologies, and skilled personnel

necessary to access these sites. Even if these equipment and personnel are available, the sheer size of some MPAs make the collection of this information very difficult.

Although marine protected areas present some special challenges for measurement of public use, there are options that do not require regular monitoring of recreation and tourism attractions within the MPA. The following sections provide general guidelines for measurement of public use, and some methods that have been used successfully with MPAs and associated coastal regions.

7.4 GENERAL GUIDELINES FOR MARINE PROTECTED AREAS

The following steps can be viewed as general guidelines in the PROCESS of measuring public use at MPAs. Please consult other chapters of this document for further guidance on these topics:

1. Develop the administrative and financial capacity for measurement and monitoring of public use

2. Define the purposes for which the information will be used

3. Define the operational boundaries of the MPA (these may be smaller than the legally designated boundaries)

4. Define the visitor populations to be measured for use

5. Determine target levels of validity and reliability (i.e., what should be measured and the quality of results)

6. Develop a design or plan for measurement of public use

7. Select appropriate methods of data collection and analysis

8. Integrate the results in management plans and activities

7.5 POTENTIAL METHODS FOR MEASUREMENT OF PUBLIC USE

The following methods have been used with varying degrees of success to measure public use of marine protected areas or associated coastal regions. The information provided on these methods is NOT intended to be a comprehensive or detailed analysis. Instead, it should be viewed as a starting point for discussion about the systematic and scientific measurement of public use of MPAs.

Prior to implementation of these methods, each MPA needs to assess its particular purposes for management, characteristics of use, available equipment and personnel, and other information to determine which method or combination of methods will be most effective and efficient for the management organization. The information derived from this assessment should be made part of a written plan for measurement of public use. Please consult this document and other sources in park planning and management for further details about preparing plans for measurement of public use.

1. VISITOR ENTRY PERMITS

    A nearly complete census of public use may be possible with the requirement to obtain a visitor permit upon each entry to the MPA. Permit information may include visitor demographics, mode of access, expected travel plans within the MPA, expected recreation activities, and other information. There may also be a requirement to present the permit to management authorities upon exit from the MPA with corrections to indicate ACTUAL travel and activities within the MPA. This method may provide the highest quality of data, but will probably inconvenience the visitor unless there are ample facilities and personnel to process permits. In addition, there could be undocumented use of the MPA by those that do NOT obtain permits.

2. ANNUAL VISITOR PERMITS

    An accurate count of annual visitors may be possible with the requirement to obtain a visitor permit upon FIRST entry of the year to the MPA. Visitors are not required to obtain permits during subsequent visits during the year. This method may provide high quality information about annual visitors, but does not allow estimation of total visitation, length of stay, or more specific patterns of use needed in resource management and development. This method is more convenient for visitors who expect to make multiple visits to the MPA during the year.

3. RATIO-BASED ESTIMATION OF VISITATION

    Annual visitation can be estimated for certain recreation activities where ratios of use can be developed between an easily measured segment of a visitor group and other segments of the group. An example is visitation by recreational scuba divers aboard charter vessels based within or near the MPA, and visitation by recreational divers aboard private or rental boats. Charter operators may be willing to provide information about visitation to the MPA as a requirement of their permit or by voluntary agreement. Occasional surveys of private/rental boat operators would provide information on the visitation of recreational scuba divers aboard non-charter vessels. A comparison of visitation aboard charter vessels and private/rental boats would provide ratios and other bases of comparison between these segments. These ratios could be used to estimate total visitation when only the visitation aboard charter vessels is known. The stability of these ratios need to be evaluated periodically to maintain the accuracy of public use estimates. The steps in developing such a method include the following:

    ▶ Complete an inventory of dive charter operations

    ▶ Determine visitation aboard charter vessels

▶ Conduct on-site surveys to estimate non-charter visitation

▶ Develop ratios for visitation over time

▶ Estimate total visitation

The surveys of non-charter vessels could include information on visitor demographics, recreation activities, and other information. Charter operators may also be willing to participate in survey of their passengers under certain conditions.

4. ON-SITE SURVEYS

Visitors of marine protected areas can be asked to complete self-administered questionnaires, or to take part in interviews about their recreation and tourism activities. On-site surveys should be designed to obtain a representative sample of visitor groups to the MPA during a certain period of time (usually seasonal and annual). These surveys usually require trained personnel who directly interact with visitors at predetermined locations within or near the marine protected area. Locations for on-site surveys include facilities, attractions, and access points such as visitor centers, marinas, boat launches, bait and tackle shops, dive sites, and fishing areas. The administration of surveys at fishing areas,

dive sites, or other places of active recreation is often viewed as an inconvenience by visitors.

If properly designed, on-site surveys can provide high quality information on many dimensions of visitor use. The collection of COMPREHENSIVE information on public use by on-site survey may not be feasible due to cost and the logistical requirements of the sampling schedule.

5. AERIAL SURVEYS OF VISITOR ACTIVITY

Aerial surveys may provide information on visitor activities within MPAs. In particular, aerial surveys can determine the number of vessels moored or anchored at certain sites (e.g., coral reefs, shipwrecks), vessels in transit within certain geographic zones, and the probable activities in which these vessels are engaged (e.g., recreational fishing, commercial fishing, snorkeling/scuba diving). This information would be available only for a point in time, unless regular aerial surveys are completed during different times of the day, days of the week, and months of the year. In addition, the accuracy of information is dependent upon the ability of survey personnel to distinguish the different types of

Guided Tour at Heron Island in the Great Barrier Reef Marine Park, Australia

People who visit parks are usually very interested in park management and are willing to give their time to assist managers by providing personal opinions on surveys.

vessels and visitor activities sometimes from great distances. Aerial surveys can be supplemented by on-site surveys to verify the accuracy of aerial observations, and to collect additional public use information. In many cases, information on the density and patterns of various uses can be developed from aerial surveys and plotted on maps, or incorporated into geographic information systems (GIS).

6. REGIONAL EXIT SURVEY
Visitor exit surveys can be conducted when COMPREHENSIVE information is needed on public use of a marine protected area or coastal region. The efficiency of such surveys is increased greatly if there are limited exit points from a MPA or coastal region. This method would probably NOT be practical for MPAs or coastal regions having numerous entry and exit points (i.e., relatively "open" access) by visitors.

An exit survey of recreation and tourism on a regional basis (including a number of marine protected areas) was recently conducted in the Florida Keys and Florida Bay region of the United States of America. In this case, exit interviews were an efficient survey method because of the limited travel routes into and out of the region (i.e., one highway, two airports, one cruise ship dock).

The survey of visitors to the region included (1) exit interviews with mailback questionnaires, and (2) supplementary interviews at over 200 sites within the region (e.g., accommodations, recreation facilities, tourism attractions). The exit interviews provided visitor profiles, estimates of trip expenditures, an understanding of the importance/satisfaction of facilities and natural resource attributes, perceptions on the state of the resource, and an indication of environmental concern. The on-site interviews provided estimates on intensity of use and net economic use values. The economic analysis

of data from the study provided estimates of both market (economic impacts) and non-market recreational use values. In addition, the study interpreted visitor perceptions of the facilities, attractions, and natural environments that support these recreational use values.

7. REGIONAL LODGING SURVEY
A scientific survey of recreation and tourism is difficult in "open" coastal areas of a region due to logistical difficulties in obtaining representative samples of participants/users. The cost of comprehensive on-site surveys is a barrier to obtaining an adequate number of responses; this in turn limits the development of valid profiles of different visitor groups and market segments within visitor groups. Overall, the complexity of logistics and high costs make it difficult to obtain reliable estimates of total use/participation for purposes of expanding survey estimates (e.g., average spending per boating day x total number of boating days). Due in large part to these constraints, there have been few comprehensive and simultaneous studies of different types of recreation and tourism, and their economic impacts within a coastal region.

An alternative to extensive on-site survey of recreation and tourism is a regional lodging survey. This alternative may reduce the complexity of logistics and costs in developing COMPREHENSIVE information on public use of a MPA or other coastal region. The effectiveness and efficiency of this method is dependent on the support of hospitality businesses in the region. An outline for design of a lodging survey is presented as follows:

RECREATION AND TOURISM SUPPLY
▶ inventory lodging facilities to determine overnight capacity and occupancy (e.g., motels, resorts, bed and breakfasts, seasonal homes, campgrounds, marina slips);

▶ inventory recreation and tourism attractions, facilities, services, and programs within shorelands of the region using EXISTING secondary data sources, aerial photos, land use maps, GIS information, and on-site validation; and

▶ develop descriptive totals of coastal recreation and tourism supply.

RECREATION AND TOURISM ACTIVITY

▶ conduct visitor surveys at overnight lodging facilities to estimate tourism-related recreation activity and spending in the local area;

▶ conduct household telephone and/or mail surveys to estimate local recreation activity and spending (i.e., permanent and seasonal residents);

▶ conduct on-site surveys at selected coastal recreation attractions and facilities to validate visitor surveys at lodging facilities, and to estimate day-use; and

▶ apply survey results to inventory data with spreadsheet models.

ECONOMIC IMPACT

▶ estimate total spending by coastal residents and visitors;

▶ apply spending data to local input-output (I-O) models to estimate economic impact; and

▶ interpret findings for local decision-makers.

FINAL PRODUCTS

▶ Descriptive inventory of overnight lodging facilities;

▶ comprehensive and descriptive inventory of recreation and tourism supply (i.e., attractions, facilities, services, programs) within the coastal region;

▶ person days of participation in various recreation activities within the region by market segments defined by the type of lodging (i.e., household, seasonal home, motel, campground) and day-trip use;

▶ importance of coastal recreation facilities, services, and environmental attributes to

participants, and their satisfaction after participation;

▶ spending profiles for specific market segments by major activities (total spending would be estimated by multiplying per day spending profiles by numbers of days within segments); and

▶ economic impact of recreation and tourism spending, estimated in terms of sales, income, and jobs for both direct and secondary impacts (i.e., indirect and induced).

Consultation with specialists is generally required to complete reliable economic analyses such as assessment of economic impacts. In some cases, computer models are available that can aid in analysis of economic impacts.

For further information on marine protected areas worldwide, consult the following publication:

Kelleher, G., C. Bleakley, and S. Welles. 1995. A global representative system of marine protected areas. Great Barrier Reef Marine Park Authority, The World Bank, and the World Conservation Union (IUCN). IUCN @ www.iucn.org

Heron Island Ferry,
Great Barrier Reef Marine Park, Australia

Private tourism operators are often very willing to cooperate with park managers in coordinated, tourism market analysis.

CHAPTER 8

THE EVOLUTION OF THE BEST PRACTICE GUIDELINES

The GUIDELINES FOR PUBLIC USE MEASUREMENT AND REPORTING AT PARKS AND PROTECTED AREAS must continue to develop. The goal is to translate them into as many languages as possible and to distribute them widely. New measurement equipment, new computer hardware and new computer software will appear. As further experience is gained, the GUIDELINES will be refined.

In order to provide as much assistance to park managers as possible, it is important that these changes be made known. For the foreseeable future, paper reports will continue to have an important role. However, reports are costly to produce and to distribute. They can go out of date quickly. With the onset of the world wide web and electronic documents, a dynamic new method for the distribution of information is now available. The WCPA's Task Force on Tourism and Protected Areas will continue to develop the existing web site. Amended reports and new technologies can be posted on this site and made available quickly. This method is inexpensive, compared to printing and mailing reports. However, it is only available to those with web access. Trends suggest that more and more park agencies and individuals in those agencies will gain web access over time.

Comments on the contents of the GUIDELINES, new technologies available and suggested improvements in public use measurement are encouraged. Case studies on the application of the GUIDELINES are encouraged and will be published as they become available. The GUIDELINES are intended to be part of a dynamic process aimed as encouraging best practice in public use measurement and reporting in parks and protected areas globally.

An important goal of these GUIDELINES is to provide a common base for measurement. Once this is in place, it enables a much more comprehensive understanding of the volume of public use of the world's parks and protected areas. The authors of these GUIDELINES hope that in the future a global, ongoing inventory and reporting of the world's park visitation will be undertaken, probably in concert with the data collection for the U. N. List of National Parks and Protected Areas. All readers of the GUIDELINES are encouraged to collect and manage the public use data of the parks and protected areas in their jurisdiction so this data can be agglomerated with data from other sites to achieve the larger picture of public use.

APPENDICES

Appendix 1

INTERNATIONAL TOURISM TERMINOLOGY

A strong statistical base is essential for a good understanding by governments, industries, academia and the public of tourism's contribution to the social, cultural and economic development of a country. For the comparison of tourism measurements in different jurisdictions, it is important for standard definitions to be used. Below are the standard tourism definitions accepted by the United Nations' Statistical Commission.

TOURISM: the activities of persons travelling to and staying in places outside their usual environment for not more than one consecutive year for leisure, business and other purposes.

DOMESTIC TOURISM: involving residents of a given country travelling only within their own country.

INBOUND TOURISM: involving non-residents visiting a country other than their own country. It is essential to classify visitors by country of residence rather than by nationality.

NATIONALITY: the government issuing the passport (or other identification document), even if the person normally resides in another country.

OUTBOUND TOURISM: involving residents travelling in another country.

INTERNAL TOURISM: comprises domestic and inbound tourism.

NATIONAL TOURISM: comprises domestic tourism and outbound tourism.

INTERNATIONAL TOURISM: consists of inbound and outbound tourism.

INTERNATIONAL VISITOR: any person who travels to a country other than that in which he has his usual residence but outside his usual environment for a period not exceeding 12 months and whose main purpose of visit is other than the exercise of an activity remunerated from within the country visited.

DOMESTIC VISITOR: any person who resides in a country, who travels to a place within the country, outside his usual environment for a period not exceeding 12 months and whose main purpose of visit is other than the exercise of an activity remunerated from within the place visited.

OVERNIGHT VISITORS: visitors who stay at least one night in a collective or private accommodation in the place visited.

This definition includes cruise passengers who arrive in a country on a cruise ship and return to the ship each night to sleep on board even though the ship remains in port for several days. Also included in this group are owners or passengers of yachts and passengers on a group tour accommodated in a train.

SAME-DAY VISITORS: visitors who do not spend the night in a collective or private accommodation in the place visited.

TOURISM EXPENDITURE: the total consumption expenditure made by a visitor or on behalf of a visitor for and during his or her trip and stay at a destination.

THE OVERALL REFERENCE IS:
United Nations and World Tourism Organization. 1994. Recommendations on Tourism Statistics. Department for Economic and Social Information and Policy Analysis, Statistical Division, Statistical Papers, Series M, No. 83.

To obtain the full report, titled Recommendations on Tourism Statistics, contact the World Tourism Organization at omt@worldtourism.org. The report presents a conceptual framework, classification system and an overview of future challenges.

Appendix 2

Attendance Methodology Form

Each park posts different challenges for the collection of public use data. In order to keep track of the variety of data collection methodologies being used across a entire agency or country, is necessary for central office managers to understand the field situations. Parks Canada developed a standard form, filled out by visitor management specialists in the field, that documents the situation in each park. Below is an example of such a form from Jasper National Park.

Park/Site	Jasper National Park				
Description of Methodology used to obtain Person-Visits[1]	Person visit stats are calculated from the traffic counters located at the East Gate, West Gate and at Jonas Creek on the Icefield Parkway. This data is collected by a contractor and sent to the Park approximately every three months. Traffic is calculated as having 2.36 passengers per vehicle and of those total passengers 0.63833 are actually visiting the Park.				
This methodology has been in effect since what year?			March 1996		
Is the methodology based upon paid visitation only?		Yes		No	XX
Confidence Level[2] of Person-Visit Methodology	Low		Medium	XX	High	
Future Improvements that can be made to the Person-Visit Methodology	Currently conducting a recalibration survey at the entrance gates. This recalibration survey will be completed in October 1999.				
Does your methodology currently require a review to ensure that it is still valid?		Yes See above comment.	XX	No	
Number of Park/Site Visitor Entry Points		Single		Multiple	XX
Annual Conversion Factor from Person-Visits to	Person-Entries[3] (All Parks/Sites)	156%	Person-Visit-Days[1] (National Parks)	100%	Person-Visit-Hours[4] (Historic Sites)	
General Note to be included with Information Requests[6]					

Comments	
Contact Person for Attendance Data	David Kjorven
Phone Number	403-852-6109
Form Completed By (Name/Title)	David Kjorven A / Frontcountry Manager
Date Completed	November 5, 1998

DEFINITION OF TERMS USED ON THE PARKS CANADA ATTENDANCE METHODOLOGY FORM:

[1]PERSON-VISIT: [2]PERSON-ENTRY
(a measure of loading on the park)
A person-entry occurs each time a person enters a reporting unit regardless of the purpose of the entry.

[3]PERSON-VISIT-DAY
(includes visitors staying overnight — a measurement used in national parks and historic canals)
A person-visit-day occurs for each day or any part thereof that a person stays in a reporting unit for the purposes of heritage appreciation or recreation.

[4]PERSON-VISIT-HOUR
(a measurement used mainly for historic sites)
A person-visit-hour occurs when a person stays in a reporting unit for one hour.

[5]CONFIDENCE LEVEL

Low	May require surveys, report cards, Point of Sale (P.O.S.) data to improve confidence level
Medium	Measurable improvements to methodology may still be possible
High	Only minor improvements can be achieved by revising methodology

[6]GENERAL NOTE
A park/site can include a general note to accompany any requests for data. The note might, for example, explain that the park has an extremely high percentage of campers that stay in the park for an average of 3 days or 2 nights. Under the person-visit unit of count they would only be counted once, however under the person-visit-day count they would be counted for each day in the park. The note would help to inform users of the data about the unique characteristics of visitors to the park or site.

Appendix 3

BENT'S OLD FORT NATIONAL HISTORIC SITE
TRIP FACT SHEET

Home Zip Code: ___ ___ ___ ___ ___
   Or Country: _____

Number of people in your vehicle visiting the park on this trip:
_____Adults (17 & over) _____Children (16 & younger)

Left Home On:_____/____/_____
           (Month/Day/Year)

Arrive LaJunta/Las Animas Area: _____/___/_____
                                (Month/Day/Year)

Arrive Park: _____/___/_____   _____:_____
            (Month/Day/Year)   (Time AM or PM)

Number of Nights Spent In The LaJunta/
Las Animas Area While On This Trip In:
   Campgrounds Outside Park _____Nights
   Hotel/Motel Outside Park _____Nights
   With Friends Outside Park _____Nights
   Did not spend the night in the area _____

Activities in Park (Check all that apply)
___ Not Visiting   ___ Sightseeing
___ Visited Park Exhibit(s) ___ Picnicking
___ Park Employee Guided Tour ___ Nature Trail
___ Self Guided Visit   ___ Special Park Event
___ Viewed Park Video/Movie ___ Take Pictures, Videos
___ Other _____

Park Entrance By (Check One)
   ___1 Cash Fee Payment   ___4 Golden Eagle Pass
   ___2 Golden Age Pass   ___5 No Fee Paid box
   ___3 Golden Access Pass ___6 Left money in donation box
            ___7 Other _____

Daily Expenditures For Your Group While In The LaJunta/Las Animas Area:
      $_____Lodging $_____Transportation
      $_____Meals $_____Miscellaneous

Leave Park for Last Time On: _____/___/_____   _____
                             (Month/Day/Year)   (Time AM or PM)

Leave LaJunta/Las Animas Area On: _____/___/_____
                                  (Month/Day/Year)

Returned Home On: _____/___/_____
                  (Month/Day/Year)

Don Hill, Superintendent
Bent's Old Fort National Historic Si[...]

Appendix 4

VISITOR SATISFACTION MEASUREMENT FEEDBACK

It is important to provide feedback to the population who are involved in service satisfaction studies. Such feedback provides the visitor with an indication that visitor surveys are taken seriously, and cause real changes in operations. The feedback also encourages visitors to participate in the next round of service monitoring. Below is one-page feedback note for the campers in the national parks of western Canada. The page is mounted on campground bulletin boards for the viewing by the campers.

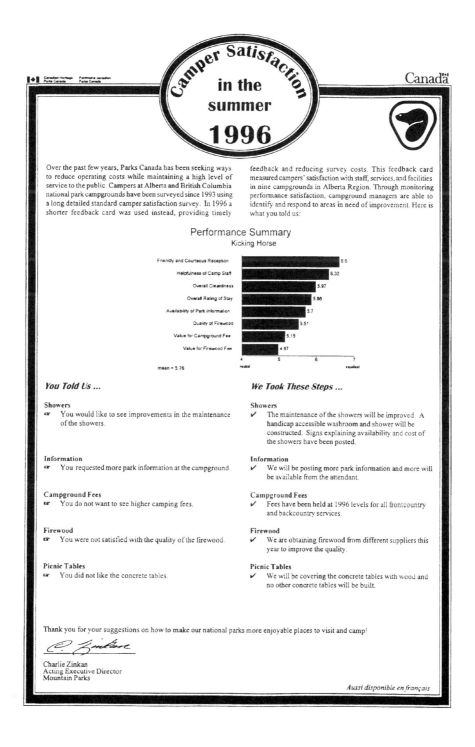

Appendix 5

GRAND TETON — Interview Location: (Jackson Lk/Pacific Crk/Deadmans/Moose/WilsonBrdg/RIVER)

SNAKE RIVER SURVEY — Interview Date: Mo   /Day   Period: (am / md / pm),   Intitals_____

8. What type of **GROUP** are you with on the river today? (Check one)

     ( )   Commercial Scenic   ( )   Private Scenic

     ( )   Commercial Fishing   ( )   Private Fishing

---

9. Please grade the park for **CROWDEDNESS** where A + = least crowded,... F = most crowded, (0 for Not Used) at:

_____ Parking Areas   _____ Visitor Centers   _____ Interpretive Programs   _____ Campgrounds

_____ Scenic Turnouts   _____ Snake River   _____ Hiking Trails   Other:_____

---

10. Did you **CHANGE** your plans due to crowded conditions? ( ) No ( ) Yes, where?_____

---

11. What should the park emphasize as it prepares for the **FUTURE**? (Rank 1st, 2nd, 3rd)

_____ Facilities

_____ Preservation

_____ Ranger Services

12. For #1 Preparation Emphasis (Fac/Pres/Rgr Srv), what do you have in mind?

    ( ) Camping   ( ) Historic Resources   ( ) Educational Act.

    ( ) Roads/Parking   ( ) Natural Resources   ( ) Info/Orientation

    ( ) Trails   ( ) Scenic Views   ( ) Ranger Patrols

    ( ) Launch/Take-out   Other:_____

---

13. Would you support **RESTRICTIONS** on your own uses of the park for *less crowded* conditions?

    ( ) Yes

               ( ) No (go to 6b.)

               ( ) DK (go to 6b.)

     6b. How about restrictions to *better preserve* the resource?

        ( ) Yes   ( ) No   ( ) DK

---

14. There may be several **ALTERNATIVES** for controlling numbers

Please rate these options:	Strongly Favor	Mildly Favor	Neither	Mildly Oppose	Strongly Oppose	DK
Additional User Fee	SF	MF	N	MO	SO	DK
Quotas	SF	MF	N	MO	SO	DK
Permit System	SF	MF	N	MO	SO	DK
Limit Future Facilities	SF	MF	N	MO	SO	DK

---

15. How would you rate your **SKILL** at

	expert	intermediate	novice
Fishing			
Floating			

16. How **OFTEN** have you floated the river as

passenger	oarsman
(trips)	(trips)

---

17. Were any areas of the river **CROWDED**?

    ( ) No

    ( ) Launch Areas

    ( ) Parking

    ( ) River

18. Did that **AFFECT** your experience?

    ( ) No Effect

    ( ) Positive

    ( ) Slightly Negative (go to 11b.)

    ( ) Extremely negative (go to 11b.)

11b. Did you

    ( ) Cut Your Stay Short

    ( ) Move Elsewhere

---

19. Anybody in your group require **SPECIAL ACCOMMODATIONS** because of physical limitations?

    ( ) No   ( ) Yes (go to 12b.)

     12b. Were the facilities adequate?

        ( ) Yes   ( ) NO

20. What YEAR were you born? 19___

21. Your residential ZIP CODE_____

               or COUNTRY_____

Is there anything else about your visit you would like park management to know about?_____

Appendix 6

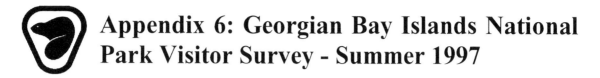

Appendix 6: Georgian Bay Islands National Park Visitor Survey - Summer 1997

Day-Use Area Survey

Introduction

This report presents the results of a client survey that was conducted during the months of July and August, 1997 at Georgian Bay Islands National Park. The survey was conducted at two day-use areas: Cedar Springs day-use area and at the Primitive day-use areas. The objectives of this study were:

v) to gather information on the demographic characteristics of visitors,

w) to determine satisfaction with services and facilities,

x) to determine visitors' spending patterns, including their interest in purchasing souvenirs related to the Park, and

y) to determine the importance of providing certain services and facilities on-site.

Visitors were chosen on a random basis, provided with questionnaires, and asked to complete and return the forms before leaving the day-use area.

The number of completed questionnaires (n=483) is sufficient for a 95% confidence level, with a margin of error of + or - 5. In other words, if the questionnaire was administered repeatedly to different groups of Georgian Bay Islands visitors from within the same visitor population, the results would be the same 19 times out of 20 (95%) within + or - 5%

About the Visitors

In order to gather information about the day-use area visitors, respondents were asked questions about their origin, party size and composition, age, and previous visits to the Park. As well, the survey was available in English and French, which provides the Park with an indication of the visitors' preferred language of choice for communication. As a result of this survey, 98% of respondents filled out the questionnaire in English, and 2% in French.

Table 1 outlines the results from these questions.

Table 1

About the Visitors to the

Georgian Bay Islands Day-Use Areas

	1997
	%
Origin: (n = 441)	
Ontario	91
Atlantic	0
Quebec	2
Western Canada	0
Yukon & NW Territories	0
USA	4
Other country	3
Visitor's Age: (n = 466)	
Under 6	10
6-16	21
17-34	18
35-54	36
55-64	10
65 and over	5
Party Composition: (n = 466)	
With children 16 and under	51
Adults 17 to 64 only	44
Seniors 65 and over only	2
Other	3
First Visit: (n = 416)	
No	77
Yes	23
Number of Visits in last 2 Years: (n = 357)	
0	4
1	8
2-3	28
4-5	9
more than 5	51
Questionnaire Language: (n = 252)	
English	98
French	2
Average Party Size:	4.7

Georgian Bay Islands National Park - Day-Use Area Survey

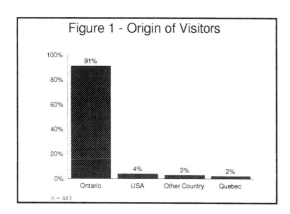

Figure 1 - Origin of Visitors

Origin

Figure 1 shows that 9 out of 10 visitor groups to the Georgian Bay Islands day-use areas live in Ontario, and only 2% came from another province in Canada (Quebec). The remaining visitors are from either the USA (4%) or another country (3%). Of those who live in Ontario, the majority come from the Central Ontario (69%) region, including Mississauga, Metro Toronto, Oshawa and Barrie.

Visitor Age and Party Composition

One key piece of information that can be derived from information about the age of people within each party is the proportion of visitors who were with children, only adults, or only seniors. These data show that over half of all parties visiting the day-use areas were made up of families (see Figure 2). Forty-four percent of all parties were made up of adults-only between ages 17 and 64

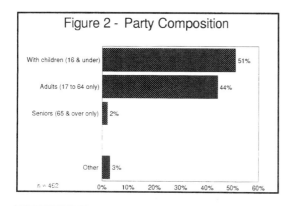

Figure 2 - Party Composition

and only 2% of all parties consisted of seniors only. The remaining 3% represents parties made up of both seniors and adults between the ages of 17- 64.

As a result of such high visitation by families, approximately one third (31%) of all visitors to the day-use areas were children 16 years old and younger, as shown in Table 1.

This information is not surprising given that many of the activities offered at the Georgian Bay Islands day-use areas are outdoor activities, and for the most part are physically engaging (e.g. boating, hiking, swimming) or are specifically targeted to families (e.g. playground, picnic, beach).

This information also reveals that the average party size for the day-use area is 4.7, which reflects the high proportion of families with children. In comparison, the average party size for parties with children is 5.5, where as the average party size for parties without children is 2.6.

Previous Visits to Park

Respondents were also asked if this was their first visit to the Georgian Bay Islands National Park (see Figure 3). A very high proportion of visitors had been to the Park before (77%).

When asked to identify the number of times they had visited the Park over the last two years, an overwhelming 51% had been back more than 5 times. Nine percent visited 4-5 times, 28% visited 2-3 times, and 8% visited just once. Only 4% of repeat visitors had not been back to the Park during the last 2 years.

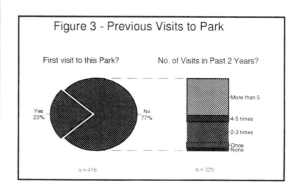

Figure 3 - Previous Visits to Park

Georgian Bay Islands National Park - Day-Use Area Survey

These data show a high rate of repeat visitation to the Park, which is a key indicator of visitor loyalty and retention. As a result, the reasons for which this group keeps coming back to this day-use area should be investigated. This information would help the Park maintain a high level of client satisfaction and will help to ensure that we are fulfilling their needs and providing them with the services and facilities they require. As well, by understanding what these visitors value and what they need, the Park will be able to manage the over-use of certain day-use areas in a more client-focused manner.

About the Visitors' Trip

Various questions were asked concerning the visitors' trip. The type of information collected included month of arrival, length of stay at the site, length of trip, type of accommodation, and how the visitors found out about the site. Please refer to Table 2 for an overview of the results.

Although there was a higher proportion of July respondents than August respondents, key statistical tests were performed on the data, and showed no significant differences in terms of visitor responses between the July sample and the August sample.

Information Source

By far, the most common source of information about the day-use areas was word of mouth from family and friends (65%). This is very positive for the Park since word of mouth is one of the most effective and least expensive means of marketing an attraction like these day-use areas. Other sources of information, although less common, were from Park publications, travel guides

and brochures, and Park staff (see Figure 4).

Table 2

About the Visitors' Trip

	1997 (%)
Month of Arrival to the Day-Use Areas: (n = 439)	
July	70
August	30
* **Information source about the Day-Use Area: (n = 436)**	
Park staff	6
Tourist information center	3
Highway signs	0
Travel guide/brochure	9
Commercial accommodation	2
Family or friends	65
Park publications	14
Road map	3
Other	18
Mode of Transportation to Day-Use Area: (n = 442)	
Car/truck with trailer	1
Car/van	1
Water taxi	3
Boat	92
Motorhome	1
Other	2
Hours in Day-Use Area: (n = 442)	
0-1 hour	4
1-2 hours	9
2-3 hours	10
3-4 hours	15
more than 4 hours	62
Average Length of Stay (in hours)	4.3
* **Services & Facilities used at the Day-Use Area: (n = 483)**	
Picnic areas/shelters	57
Walking/hiking trails	48
Viewpoints/pulloffs	25
Interpretive panels	23
Swimming/beach use	75
Washrooms	75
Parking lots	1
Nights Away from Home: (n = 459)	
0	16
1 to 3 nights	23
4 to 6 nights	15
7 or more nights	46

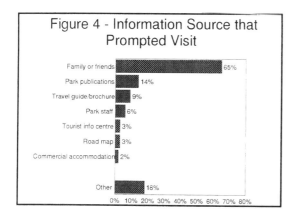

Figure 4 - Information Source that Prompted Visit

Family or friends	65%
Park publications	14%
Travel guide/brochure	9%
Park staff	6%
Tourist info centre	3%
Road map	3%
Commercial accommodation	2%
Other	18%

0% 10% 20% 30% 40% 50% 60% 70% 80%

Georgian Bay Islands National Park - Day-Use Area Survey

Word of mouth is one of the most effective and least expensive means of marketing an attraction like these day-use areas. Other sources of information, although less common, were from Park publications, travel guides and brochures, and Park staff (see Figure 4).

Mode of Transportation

Over 90% of visitors arrived at the day-use areas by privately owned boats and 3% arrived by water taxi. Given that Georgian Bay Islands N.P. is an island park with all facilities and services on the islands, it must be assumed that the respondents who indicated other modes of transportation (car/truck with trailer or a car/van) were referring to how they arrived at the Park's mainland area prior to leaving for the islands.

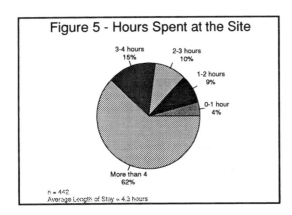

Figure 5 - Hours Spent at the Site

3-4 hours 15%
2-3 hours 10%
1-2 hours 9%
0-1 hour 4%
More than 4 62%

n = 442
Average Length of Stay = 4.3 hours

Time spent at the Site

As illustrated in Figure 5, the majority of visitors (62%) spent more than 4 hours in the day-use areas, while only 4% stayed less than 1 hour and 25% spent between 2 - 4 hours. As a result, the average length of stay at the day-use area is 4.3 hours.

Activities During Visit

Visitors were asked to identify what Park activities they had engaged in during their visit. The most common activities were swimming/beach use, boating, walking/ hiking, and enjoying a picnic (see Figure 6). Only 15% of visitors went to the Visitor Centre at Cedar Springs and only 6% participated in an interpretation programs. These low numbers for the heritage presentation services may be a result of limited knowledge of the availability of these services or programs or may be due to the distance between the day use areas and the interpretation facilities, which in some cases equates to half an hour of travel time. Further research may be considered to determine the interests and needs of these

visitors in order to encourage more participation in heritage presentation programs.

Table 2 (Continued)	1997 (%)
Nights Within 1 Hour of Park: (n = 368)	
0	14
1 to 3 nights	32
4 to 6 nights	19
7 or more nights	35
* Type of Accommodation: (n = 371)	
Hotel/ motel/ bed & breakfast	4
Camping	11
Friends/ relatives	3
Own cottage	7
Boat	71
Other	3
* Activities during Visit: (n = 467)	
None - passing through	2
Picnic	46
Swim/beach	82
Fish	28
Walk/hike	50
Boating	71
Interpretive activity	6
Golf	1
Canoe/kayak	3
Camp	9
Visiting a visitor centre	15

* Percent may exceed 100% due to multiple responses

Nights Away from Home & Accommodation Used

Only 16% of visitors did not plan on spending any nights away from home; 23% planned on being away between

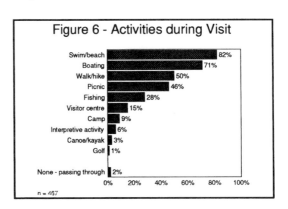

Figure 6 - Activities during Visit

Swim/beach 82%
Boating 71%
Walk/hike 50%
Picnic 46%
Fishing 28%
Visitor centre 15%
Camp 9%
Interpretive activity 6%
Canoe/kayak 3%
Golf 1%
None - passing through 2%

n = 467

Georgian Bay Islands National Park - Day-Use Area Survey

1 to 3 nights; 15% between 4 to 6 nights; and 46% for at least 7 nights. Eighty-six percent of those who planned on staying overnight chose accommodations within one hour of the Park. As indicated, the most common type of accommodation used was a boat (71%), followed by camping (11%), and use of visitors' own cottage (7%).

How Well are We Doing?

Based on their current visit, respondents were asked to rate the performance of Parks Canada at Georgian Bay Islands, using a list of facilities and services offered at the day-use areas. They were asked to use a 5-point scale, where 1=very poorly and 5=very well. Table 3 outlines the results of this question. Please note, the percentages shown in the table do not include visitors who did not use the service or facility in question.

Satisfaction Ratings

> ### TOP BOX ANALYSIS
>
> *Top-Box theory maintains that the only completely satisfied clients are the ones who check the "top box" in a survey (e.g. "5" on a scale of 1 to 5). Anything less than the top box means that there was something the respondent was dissatisfied with. Top-Box theory also advocated that between 40% and 60% of scores should land in the top box if a company is doing a good job of completely satisfying its clients. Results for these day-use areas are presented on this and the subsequent page.*

Satisfaction With Georgian Bay Islands Day-Use Area Services and Facilities

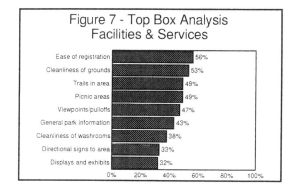

Figure 7 - Top Box Analysis
Facilities & Services

Ease of registration	56%
Cleanliness of grounds	53%
Trails in area	49%
Picnic areas	49%
Viewpoints/pulloffs	47%
General park information	43%
Cleanliness of washrooms	38%
Directional signs to area	33%
Displays and exhibits	32%

As indicated in Figure 7, over 40% visitors were very satisfied (rating this service or facility a "5" out of "5") with ease of registration, cleanliness of grounds, trails and picnic areas, viewpoints/pulloffs, and general Park information. However, only 32% of visitors were completely satisfied with displays and exhibits.

Table 3: Levels of Satisfaction

	Very Well 5	4	3	2	Very Poorly 1	n
Services & Facilities						
Trails in area	49	38	12	1	0	358
Picnic areas	49	40	10	1	0	404
Viewpoints/ pulloffs	47	37	13	2	1	315
Directional signs to area	33	30	24	8	5	363
Displays and exhibits	32	33	27	7	1	344
Cleanliness of grounds	53	34	10	2	1	452
Cleanliness of washrooms	38	38	16	5	3	422
Ease of registration	56	29	10	20	5	432
General park information	43	35	17	3	2	440
Staff						
Friendliness	68	24	7	0	1	463
Availability	27	30	25	12	6	437
Responsiveness	42	33	18	4	3	424
Overall Visit						
As educational experience	24	39	27	8	2	315
As recreational experience	57	34	7	2	0	438
As fun for children	56	31	11	1	1	326
Value for dollar	41	30	17	8	4	421

Satisfaction With Georgian Bay Islands Day-Use Area Staff

Staff at Georgian Bay Islands can be commended for their friendliness to visitors. As indicated by respondents, the friendliness of staff received the highest rating, as seen in Figure 8. Forty-two percent of visitors were very satisfied (rating a "5") with staff responsiveness to their concerns and questions.

Unfortunately, only one quarter of visitors were

Georgian Bay Islands National Park - Day-Use Area Survey

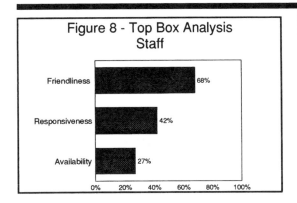

completely satisfied with the availability of staff. This concern may be explained by the limited number of staff at Georgian Bay Islands and the layout of the Park and its services. Further investigation to explain this lower score and to find ways to make staff more available to the public should be pursued.

Satisfaction With Overall Visit

As indicated in Figure 9, the day-use areas received high ratings as a recreational experience, and as fun for children, by over half the respondents. These high scores are important since half of all parties going to these areas were with children under 16. Value for dollar

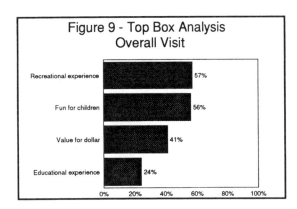

was rated fairly high, indicating a perceived high value for the fee paid. In order to ensure that this perceived value remains high the Park must deliver on the services and facilities that the visitors consider important. This is particularly important when a fee increase may be considered.

Visitors rated their overall visit as an educational experience much lower than as a recreational experience, with only 24% of visitors rating this attribute as very satisfactory. This is an indicator that the visitors to the day-use areas are interested in an educational experience, and that they are not satisfied with the perceived educational services and facilities available to them. As indicated previously, this may be due to a lack of awareness of the existing programs and facilities, or it may be that the needs of the visitors are not being met. Further work must be performed in this area in order to understand the needs and values of the visitors for the fulfillment of an educational experience.

Specific Issues

Importance of Various Services and Facilities

A key component of satisfying of customers is ensuring that the services and facilities they feel are important are provided to them. Therefore, in an effort to understand what services and facilities are important to Georgian Bay Islands visitors, respondents were asked to rate on a scale from 1 (not at all important) to 5 (very important), how important it is that a number of facilities and services be provided to them at the day-use area. Table 4 outlines these results.

Table 4

Level of Importance of Providing Services/Facilities at the Georgian Bay Islands Day-Use Areas

	Very Important			Not Important		
	5	4	3	2	1	n
FACILITIES						
Change houses	21	11	13	10	45	417
Picnic shelters	38	21	18	7	16	415
Picnic tables	67	20	8	2	3	450
Fireplaces	40	19	16	10	15	429
Docking facilities	79	8	6	2	5	452
Walking/hiking trails	42	29	20	4	5	425
Buoyed swimming areas	29	16	19	12	24	423
SERVICES						
Children's playground	27	17	20	11	25	419
Interpretive services	13	16	26	12	33	409
Visitor centre	18	24	29	12	17	416
Outdoor theater program	14	18	25	15	28	411
Guided walks	11	13	26	16	34	413
Staff available on site	29	17	21	11	22	423
Interpretive activities for children	17	15	22	15	31	408
General park info	34	25	29	7	5	425
Info about Parks Canada	22	23	28	13	14	411

Georgian Bay Islands National Park - Day-Use Area Survey

Facilities

The facilities which visitors indicated to be most important to provide were docking facilities and picnic tables. Other facilities of importance to provide are walking/hiking trails, fireplaces and picnic shelters. Visitors did not think that it was important to provide buoyed swimming areas and change houses.

Providing Services

Of highest importance to visitors was the provision of general Park information. Visitors also felt it was very important to have staff available on site. Given that visitors were not very satisfied with staff availability, Parks Canada must look into this concern and find ways to make staff more available.

Heritage presentation programs and services such as outdoor theatre, interpretive services, and guided walks were not indicated as being important. Further work should be undertaken to determine why interest in these programs is so low and how this can be changed.

Interest in Purchasing Souvenirs

Visitors were given a list of souvenirs depicting Georgian Bay Islands National Park, and their corresponding selling price (see table below). They were then asked to indicate which souvenirs they were likely to purchase if available at the Park.

Souvenir Options	
Postcard ($0.50)	Souvenir spoon ($10)
Large site map ($5)	Navigation charts ($20)
Topographic map ($5)	Poster ($4)
Book ($10)	CD Rom ($50)

As indicated, close to one-third of respondents were not interested in purchasing any souvenirs (see Figure 10). Those who expressed interest in purchasing items leaned towards postcards (24%), navigational charts (23%), large site maps (18%), and topographic maps (17%). There is some interest in posters and books, but very little interest for souvenir spoons and CD Rom's.

Amount Spent in Local Area

Thirty percent of all visitors spent less than $50 in the local area, which in the survey is defined as within one hour of the Park. However, more than one quarter of visitors, as seen in Figure 11, spent over $300 in the local area. As a result, Georgian Bay Islands visitors contribute significantly to the local economy.

A logical next step for future research at this Park would be to determine what this money is being spent on, in an effort to enhance our understanding of the economic

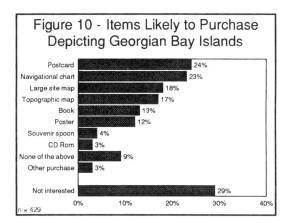

Figure 10 - Items Likely to Purchase Depicting Georgian Bay Islands

impact of these users on the area.

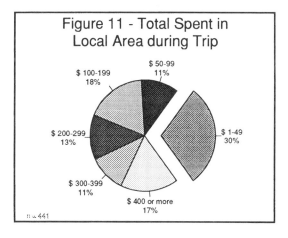

Figure 11 - Total Spent in Local Area during Trip

Summary of Key Findings

There is a very high concentration of Ontario visitors to the Georgian Bay Islands day-use areas (91%); and over 70% of visitors are frequent, repeat customers. It is therefore extremely important to ensure that their experience remains highly satisfactory. In addition, word of mouth seems to be the most effective source of information to prompt the public to visit the day-use

Georgian Bay Islands National Park - Day-Use Area Survey

areas. Providing the visitor with the experience they expect, in a highly satisfactory way, will help to keep referrals from family and friends coming.

The low numbers of non-Ontario Canadians may provide Parks Canada with an opportunity to promote the Park inter-provincially, so that Canadians will visit and learn more about our system of National Parks and National Historic Sites. In order to ensure that this Park is ready to expand its market share, efforts must be made to ensure that a high level of satisfaction is being reached for facilities and services that are important to the existing visitors (this report includes information on the importance of various services and facilities as indicated by the respondent). This should be done prior to spending resources on attracting new markets to ensure that a top quality experience will be provided to them during their first visit. Failure to meet their expectations could lead to negative word-of-mouth publicity. (Note: visitation from these segments in other parts of the Park may be higher, but this survey deals strictly with the day-use areas).

Half of all parties at the day-use areas are with children 16 years old and younger. Given this percentage, Parks Canada can be commended for receiving high ratings in visitor satisfaction with their visit as a recreational experience, and as fun for children.

Only 16% of visitors did not plan on spending any nights away from home. Eighty-six percent of those who planned on staying overnight chose accommodation within one hour of the Park, and their most popular accommodation type was boat. As a result, visitors contribute significantly to the local economy, with over one quarter of visitors spending over $300 during one visit.

Visitors did not rate displays/exhibits, directional signs to the day-use area, and cleanliness of washrooms highly. It is important to further investigate these services to see if they should be improved.

Overall, staff were highly rated in terms of their friendliness and responsiveness. However, they received a less-than-satisfactory rating for availability, which gives cause for concern, since visitors felt that it was very important that staff be available when needed. Talks with staff and management would help in targeting the problem areas, and help to improve staff availability.

It will be important to continue to offer docking facilities, high quality picnic tables and shelters, well maintained trails, and fireplaces, in order to provide visitors with the facilities they expect to receive. In terms of services, providing information about the Park, a children's playground, and staff available on site should become priorities.

There is some support for the sale of souvenirs at Georgian Bay Islands National Park. Visitors were mostly interested in postcards, navigational charts, large site maps, and topographic maps. The survey did not state where the items would be sold, therefore we are unsure if the location of the sale of these items would have an effect on visitors' purchasing behavior. More research and analysis is likely needed in this regard.

Because of the high rate of repeat visitation, Parks Canada needs to carefully calculate its souvenir revenue estimates, since repeat visitors are not likely to be repeat buyers of souvenirs.